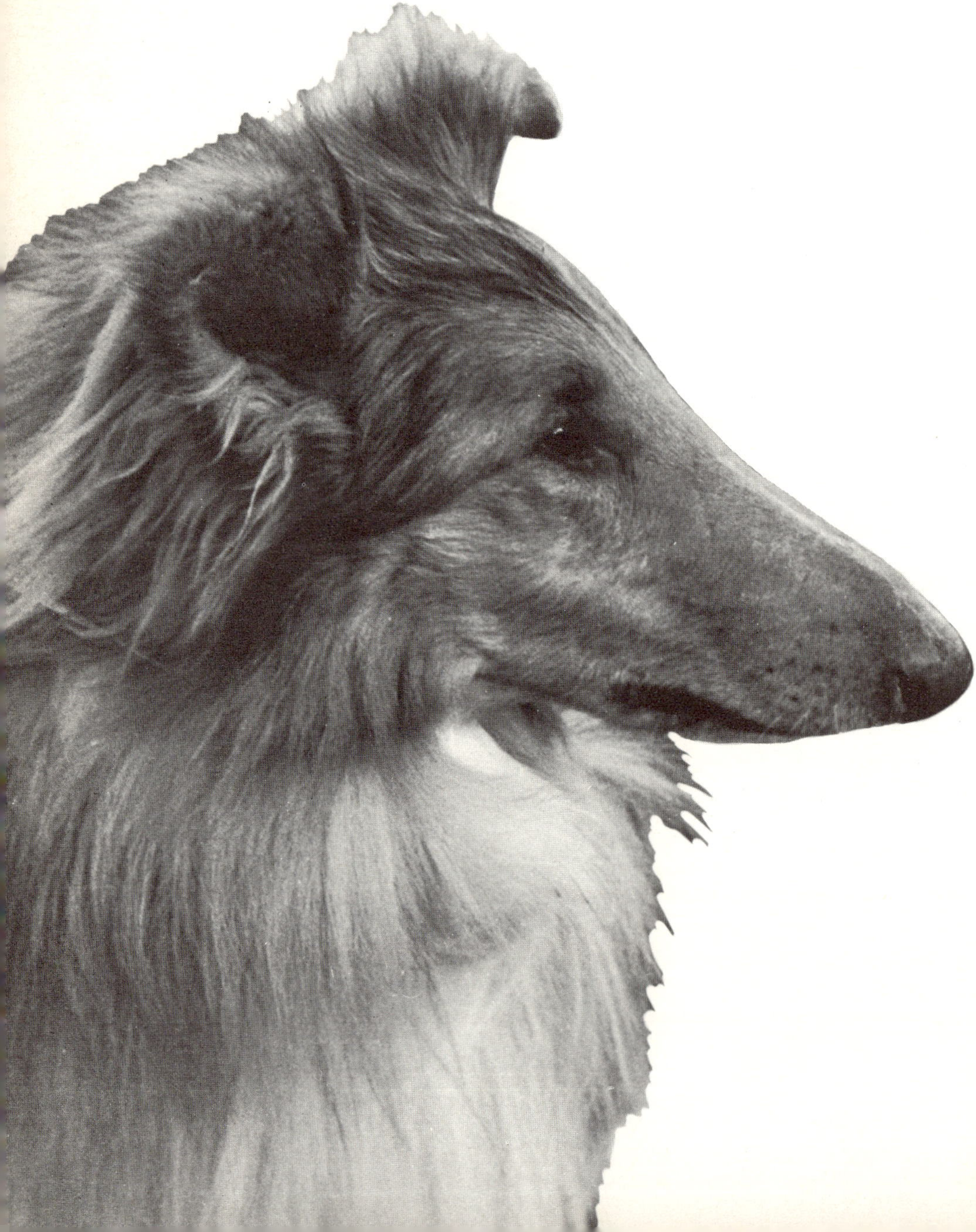

The Complete Illustrated
# COLLIE

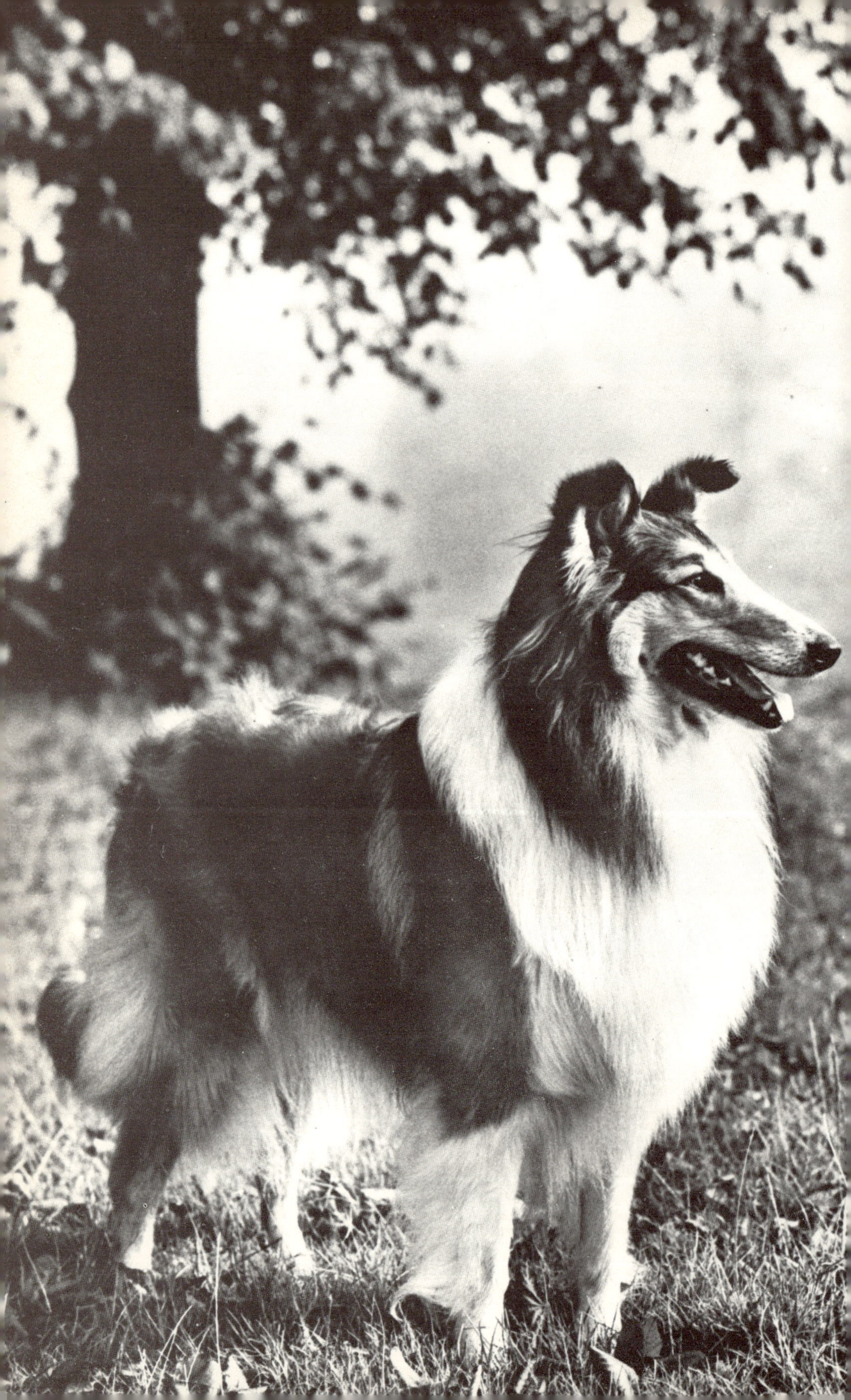

# The Complete Illustrated
# COLLIE

Edited by

## Joe and Liz Cartledge

With contributions by

JOYCE COLLIS
JOAN E. HILL
JOHN HOLMES
MARGARET OSBORNE
BETTY PENN-BULL
AILEEN SPEDING
MICHAEL STOCKMAN

Ebury Press · London

First published 1973
by Ebury Press
Chestergate House, Vauxhall Bridge Road
London SW1V 1HF

© J. H. Cartledge 1973

All rights reserved. No part of this publication may be reproduced, stored in a retrieval system, or transmitted in any form or by any means, electronic, mechanical, photocopying, recording or otherwise, without the prior permission of the copyright owner.

ISBN 0 85223 044 3

**All photographs by Angela Cavill unless otherwise indicated**

Photoset in Great Britain by
Typesetting Services Ltd, Glasgow
and printed and bound by
Interlitho s.p.a., Milan, Italy.

# Contents

1 The Collie as a Pet — *page 8*

2 The Rough Collie — *40*

3 The Smooth Collie — *46*

4 The Bearded Collie — *54*

5 Training — *72*

6 Breeding — *96*

7 Common Illnesses, Recognition and Treatment — *118*

8 Kennel Club Breed Standards — *134*

Index — *138*

# The Editors

**JOE CARTLEDGE**
It would be right to say that Joe Cartledge has been concerned with pedigree dogs and dog shows all his life. Before the First World War and between the two wars his uncle, the late Arthur Cartledge, was one of the foremost dog handlers in Britain and in the United States. It was in these surroundings and environment that Joe developed his love for the dog game. Except for his years in the services in the Second World War dogs have been his whole life, first as a boy with his uncle, and then as kennelman with the world famous Crackley Terrier Kennels. In 1949 he started his own kennels and handled dogs for many of the top people in the dog world throughout the fifties, winning championships in eleven different breeds, including Dog of the Year award on two occasions, and Best in Show with an Airedale Terrier at Cruft's, the world's most important dog show, in 1961. He retired from handling at the end of 1961 as he found that the handling of dogs both here and on the Continent, his writing and judging both in Britain and abroad he was becoming too diversified. He now judges almost every week in Britain, and has judged in Hong Kong, Ceylon, Singapore, Malaysia, Australia, New Zealand, Rhodesia, Zambia, The Republic of South Africa, Brazil, Argentina, Uruguay Finland, Sweden, Norway, Denmark, Italy, Germany, Switzerland and Holland. He contributes a weekly column in *Dog World,* the top weekly paper devoted to pedigree dogs. He is Chairman of Ryslip Kennels Ltd., and of Ryslip Livestock Shipping Company. He edits and publishes the *Dog Directory* and *Dog Diary.*

**LIZ CARTLEDGE**
Although young in years, Liz, like her husband, has also spent her entire life with dogs. She was born in Gothenburg, Sweden, to parents who were both concerned with the exhibiting and training of dogs, mainly Dobermanns and Boxers. She came to England first in 1964 as a kennel student with the Dreymin Kennels of Beagles, Bassets and Corgis. Later, and until her marriage, she was on the editorial staff of *Dog World*. A dog judge herself, she travels the world as secretary to her husband, one of the busiest judges in the world today.

# 1 The Collie as a Pet
BY AILEEN SPEDING

The Collie needs little introduction to anyone interested in dogs; from time immemorial the shepherd with his flock and his trusty Collie dog who fulfils the role of both companion and worker has illustrated the bond of affection and trust between man and dog. The present-day Collie is still capable of a good day's work and some are used regularly as trained sheep-dogs. Others have been trained as guide dogs for the blind, but most are bred for the show ring and as companions and pets.

They are strikingly handsome dogs with a long, harsh coat and a clean and smooth face. The legs have attractive featherings and the tail is long and plumed. A Collie should instantly appeal as a dog of great beauty, gifted with intelligence and alertness. But the Collie is not just a set of standards dreamed up to satisfy a whim of fashion, for every feature of the dog has evolved through his working ancestry.

As a guard dog for sheep the Collie had to be capable of great bursts of speed, jump well and change direction instantly for hours on end in extreme weather conditions. The Collie developed therefore as a tough, active and intelligent dog, fairly high on the leg for a sheep-dog, with straight front legs, well laid shoulders, a narrow pelvis to make turning easier, a rise over the loins and well-muscled thighs for jumping. He has a deep brisket, good spring of rib with plenty of room for the heart and lungs (but not barrel chested), a long body and a long low set tail. The Collie is very sure footed, with neat oval feet and well arched toes. His powerful frame is covered with a fairly long harsh outer coat and a dense cotton woolly undercoat. The outer coat forms a heavy mane over the chest and shoulder for protection against the weather, but is at no time an encumbrance – the texture keeps out the rain and snow but stays free from matts and tangles.

The head also reflects the working background of the dog; it is covered with smooth short hair which gives maximum vision and the eyes are deeply set, protecting them from gorse and brambles. Peripheral vision is good as

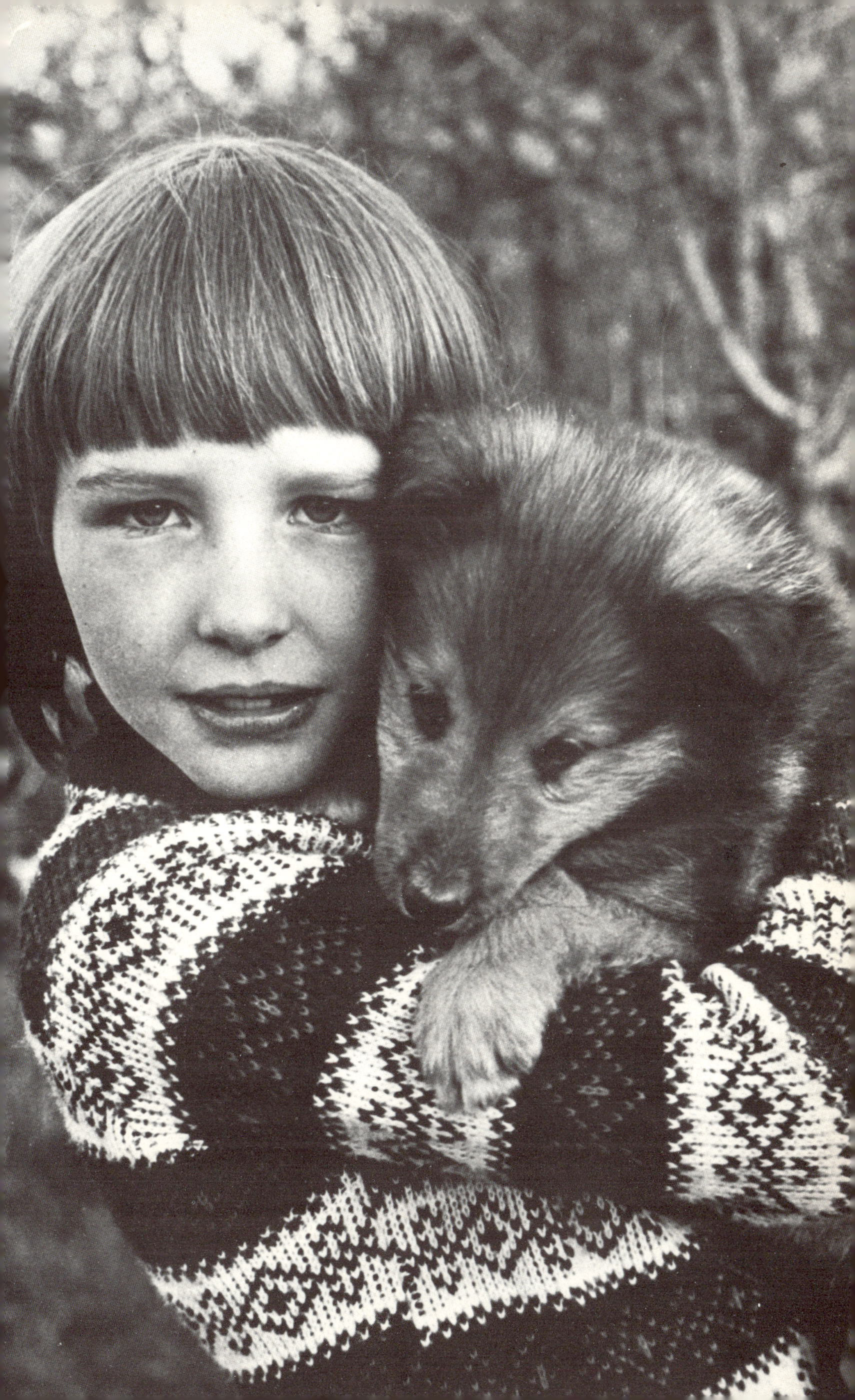

the eyes are set obliquely. The skull itself is moderately wide between the ears to allow room for the brain, and the ears are carried semi-erect to catch sound easily. The foreface is strong enough to withstand an accidental blow from a cow, horse or sheep, but the head is still fairly small for the size of the dog, making it capable of quick movement.

    These working dogs would accompany sheep to market where, presumably, the more stylish Collies caught the eye of the early dog fanciers in and around Birmingham. By the mid-nineteenth century, the dog was easily recognisable as a forerunner of the present-day Collie. At a very early dog show held in Birmingham in 1860, classes were held for 'sheep-dogs' to include Collies with both long and smooth coats.

    One of the Collie breeds' earliest devotees was S. E. Shirley, founder of the Kennel Club, who owned and bred Trefoil, a tri-colour whelped in 1873 to whom all present-day Collies can trace their ancestry in direct tail-male.

    A prospective owner of a Collie will naturally be interested in the background of his dog. The area in which he originally worked was thinly populated and harsh, and his only company would have been the shepherd and his sheep. Here the Collie acquired his deep understanding of humans, his ability to 'read thoughts' and his need for human company – indeed, without it, he becomes nervous and unsure and will not develop his high intelligence or express his character fully. His working background has formed traits of behaviour that make owning a Collie fascinating and rewarding. He is sturdily independent, never servile, capable of great loyalty and devotion but rarely openly demonstrative except to favoured members of the family – sometimes only to one person. He is instantly obedient if he can see the necessity for the command – if he can't he will be illogically stubborn. As he learns quickly but tires of repetitive lessons obedience training can be a problem. On the other hand, give a Collie a proper job with responsibility and see how effectively he acts as nurse-maid, children's escort or puppy trainer! His intelligence is not necessarily a virtue; he is an expert in one-upmanship and you as the owner must stay one step ahead. This will lead to a healthy relationship between dog and owner, and give hours of pleasure to both.

The Collie is easily house-trained as he has very clean habits. Collies are extremely fond of children – there are many true stories of Collies saving children from disasters (even Collies that are not used to children seem to be immediately happy in their presence, and also seem to have an affinity with anything young and helpless. One of our Collie bitches will 'rescue' mice that cats have caught and will sit with them between her front paws, quite oblivious of the fact that they are as terrified of her as of the cat!). Collies are very responsive to their owner's moods – happy and gay when things are going well for him, sympathetic when things are going badly and abject and humble when in disgrace for some misdemeanour.

As a guard dog he is effective but in most cases lacks real aggression. Most Collies have a good bark and will announce the presence of a stranger in no uncertain terms. He will quickly learn to recognise tradesmen and will escort the milkman or postman with a happily wagging tail, but any casual callers must pass a vigorous inspection.

Although an active dog when being exercised, at home the Collie is basically very lazy, liking nothing better than to lie in the sun or in front of the fire. He is quiet and careful indoors, rarely causing bother or knocking over ornaments or small pieces of furniture. But every Collie has one very irritating habit – he will insist on lying down in front of the particular door you want to open and will be very slow to rouse himself!

Many people are dubious about choosing a Collie as they feel the coat must need a great deal of time and attention to keep it right; this is far from true. The coat does not tangle or matt easily, and for about ten months each year needs little attention apart from weekly grooming. The annual moult does call for more vigorous attention as many hairs are lost – these are easily removable from upholstery and fabrics.

If you are thinking of buying a Collie, the first decision is whether to choose a male dog or a bitch as there is a considerable difference in size. The male Collie is a big fellow, standing between twenty-two and twenty-four inches high at the shoulder; when in full coat with his stand-off mane and frill he looks even bigger than the sixty pounds he weighs. The bitch is smaller, weighing forty to forty-five pounds, and although she grows an attractive coat with featherings and 'petticoats' she never grows the spectacular mane or length of coat the male does. Apart from size, there is little to choose between the character. Collies are home-loving and are not inclined to wander or indulge in illicit love affairs; the male Collie will be happy to mark out his home territory and patrol its boundaries daily. The bitches are rather prim and proper; when they are in season they are even more prudish and do not encourage male followers. Whether it is because of the profusion of hair on the hind quarters or because the Collie bitch is just not attractive to male dogs of any breed, the

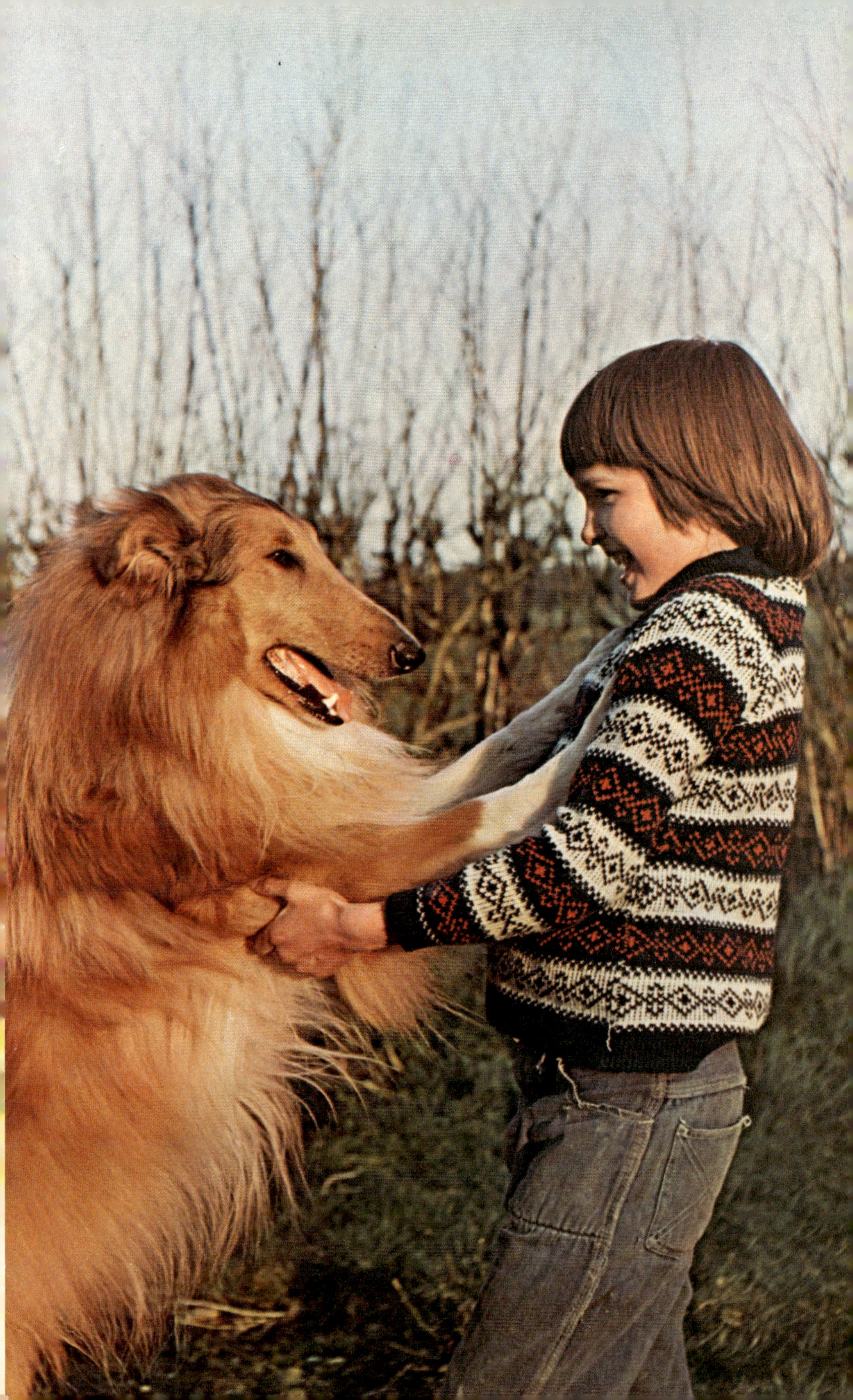

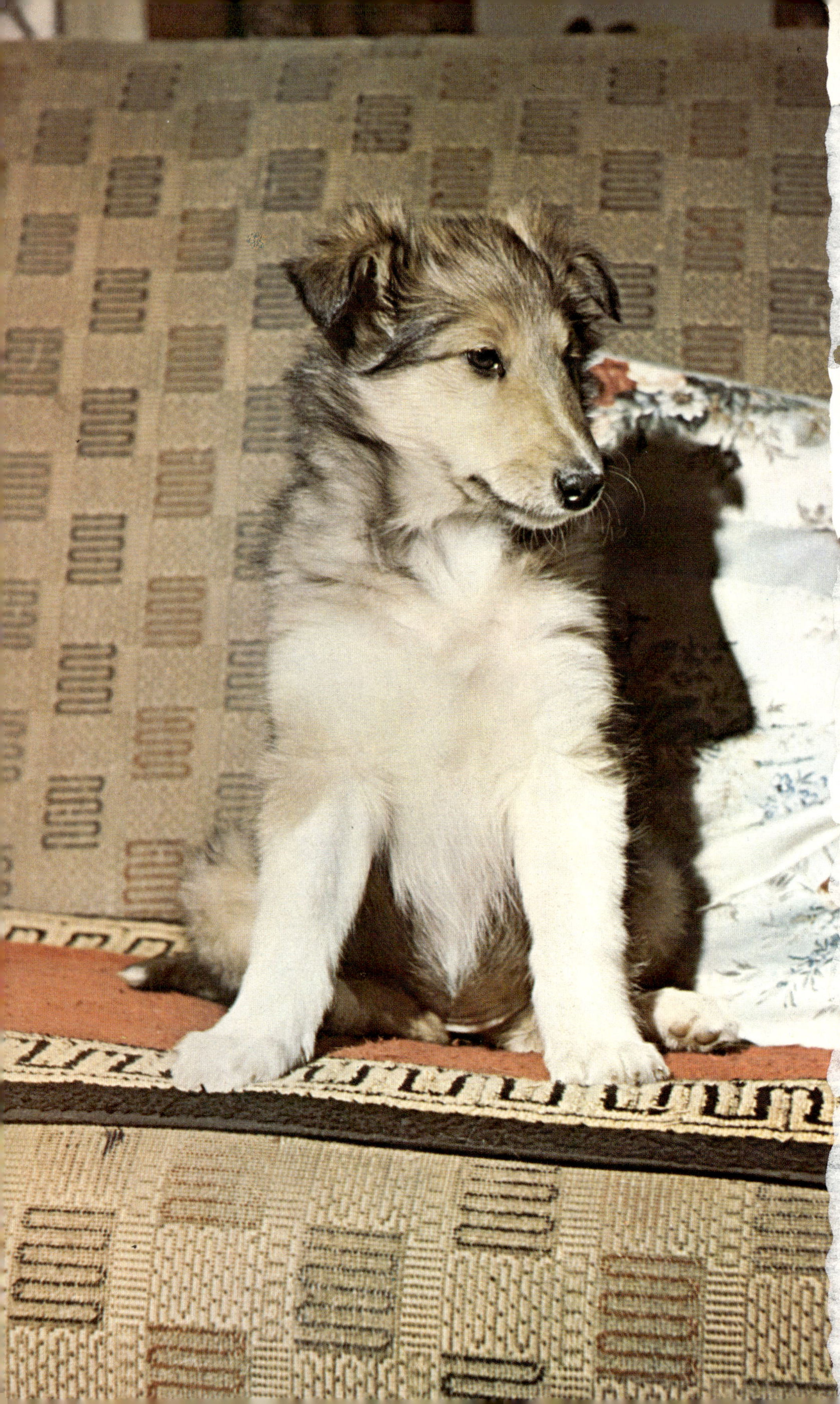

owner never seems to have a string of suitors besieging the house and garden. The Collie bitch does not come into season very often, having the first between ten and eighteen months old and subsequently at approximately yearly intervals. If she is not bred from regularly the time between season lengthens and by the age of ten she may have stopped coming into season altogether (a normal Collie bitch may well only have six or seven seasons during her life).

The next decision will be which colour to choose. There are three recognised colours, the most popular of which is sable which covers all variations of brown from pale honey to mahogany. Most sables have a framing of black on the ruff and dark shadings on the face which give a widow's peak effect, though some pale dogs have no dark shadings at all. All sables have a bar of dark hairs just below the base of the tail, and have a white tail tip.

Tri-colour is the term used for the basically black coated Collie. The coat on the body is a deep, glossy black and the head has tan markings on the cheeks and eyebrows, and there are also tan markings where black meets white on the legs.

Blue merles are less common but extremely attractive and unusual; the coat is a clear silvery blue colour splashed or marbled with black. The facial markings are tan.

Sables and tri-colours should have dark brown eyes; the blue merle has either dark brown eyes or, as is often the case, one or both eyes can be blue or blue-flecked. All three colourings can carry white Collie markings, with a white collar, shirt front, legs, feet and tail tip, or a white blaze down the face. In America, the white Collie (all white with sable, tri-colour or merle head markings) can be shown, but in Great Britain this colouring is not recognised as a true Collie colour (of course this makes no difference to them as companions).

*Breeding for Colour*
A sable can be mated to a sable or a tri-colour, and will produce only sables and tri-colours – a pair of sables can

produce a whole litter of tri-colours if both carry tri-colour genes. Two golden sables will usually produce all golden sables. Tri-colours can be mated to all three colours; with sables they produce sables and tri-colours, but mated to another tri-colour will produce all tri-colours (the only infallible fact in breeding Collies!). Tri-colour mated to merle will produce merle or tri-colour. Merles are usually mated only to tri-colours, but can be mated to another merle (there is a danger that defective white puppies without sight or hearing or both will be born and will have to be destroyed).

The final choice is between the rough coated and smooth coated Collie. Each breed has its devoted followers. The Kennel Club have now recognised the Smooth Collie as a separate breed and cross-breeding will gradually cease. The Smooth Collie's body shape is slightly different and his ears are set a little more on the side of the head – as far as looks and temperament are concerned there is little difference, and although I am writing this chapter about Rough Collies, everything mentioned will apply equally to both breeds.

*Buying a Puppy*
When you have decided to buy a Collie puppy, try to see the litter at about five to six weeks old before any have left the nest. Make sure the mother's temperament is sound; she should be friendly, and tolerant of strangers in her owner's presence even when the puppies are being handled. Left alone with visitors she may become aloof and suspicious, but should not display aggression or nervousness. It is unlikely that you will be able to see the father with the puppies unless the litter is bred by a well-known breeder, but try to see a picture of the dog, and if he lives within travelling distance make arrangements with his owner to see him, if possible, to ensure that he too has a pleasant sensible temperament.

A breeder of repute will be only too happy to give advice and help in selecting the most suitable puppy for your requirements, but if given the choice, go for a sturdy, friendly puppy with a shortish balanced head and no exaggerations such as very small eyes or a mouth that doesn't bite levelly. He should have straight front legs, strong hindquarters, a short dense coat free from signs of skin infections and a black nose, eye-rims and lips.

At seven or eight weeks old the puppy will be ready to start his new life, and adequate preparation must be made for his welfare and management. Properly brought up and cared for he will grow into a strong and healthy dog who will keep in excellent health for many years.

*Diet*
When you buy the puppy the breeder should give you a diet sheet and it is important that for the first few weeks you feed the puppy what he has been having since weaning to avoid gastric upsets. With the rest of the litter most puppies are good feeders; they know that if they don't eat up the food will disappear down the throat of a competitor. Without competition, the puppy may become fussy about food, but it is important not to make an issue of this and do not be tempted to hand-feed him. If the food is not eaten within a reasonable time, say fifteen minutes, remove it until the next feed time and either offer it again or give a different meal. Some dogs really do not like certain foods and it is a waste of time trying to get them to eat something they dislike; it is better to find an acceptable alternative the dog will eat with pleasure. Bearing all this in mind, and remembering that there are many forms in which the basic proteins and carbohydrates can be given, here is a typical rearing chart which covers the needs of a growing Collie.

Up to three months, five meals daily:–

*Morning:* Baby cereal using about 2 dessertspoons of cereal mixed to a creamy consistency with fresh milk and sweetened with a teaspoon of clear honey or glucose.

*Noon:* Two to four ounces of minced beef mixed with a slice of wholemeal bread and moistened with milk, gravy or stock.

*Afternoon:* Cereal and milk, as in the morning. For variety use a different type of cereal or a little cooked rice pudding, egg custard or scrambled egg.

*Evening:* A meat meal, as at noon.

*Bedtime:* A saucer of warm milk or proprietary milk drink. Leave a few rusks of brown bread or small dog biscuits (these will probably not be eaten, but will give the puppy something to play with or chew or if he wakes in the night or early morning).

From three to five months, three meals daily:–

*Morning:* Continue with the cereal and milk mixture as long as the puppy will eat it, using at least half a pint of milk. If he refuses, try giving the milk drink on its own and give brown bread and dripping, fried bread or toast separately. Some dogs like milky tea, others will eat cottage cheese or natural yoghourt.

*Noon:* Eight to twelve ounces of meat. Cheaper cuts and tinned food can be used. Cut raw meat into cubes about an inch square, mix with two cups of wholemeal dog meal soaked in hot stock or gravy and allowed to cool. Use whole meat tinned food. Acceptable alternatives are tinned pilchards or herrings, or fresh cooked fish, especially herrings (remove the bones when cooked).

*Evening:* A similar meal to noon.

From five to eight months:–

The maximum growth period when as much protein as possible must be given. A male Collie will require at least two pounds of meat daily and a bitch one and a half. Continue to feed a milky breakfast if the dog will eat it. Divide the meat between two meals, giving the main meal towards the evening and a slightly smaller one at mid-day. Add cereal either as biscuit meal, dog biscuits, wholemeal bread or rice; encourage a thin dog to eat as much as

Sally Anne Thompson

possible but restrict intake if he is putting on too much weight.

From eight months to a year:–

Gradually reduce the amount of meat and establish a routine of one meal a day. At a year old, the adult male Collie will be eating about one pound of meat and the bitch three-quarters, plus household scraps, biscuit meal or dog biscuits. Some adult dogs like a 'breakfast' drink of milk and a few rusks or toast.

As a breed, Collies do not seem to be able to take as much meat as some other breeds of similar size, and if your dog passes loose dark bowel actions it indicates too much meat and not enough bulk in the diet. Varying the proportion of meat and carbohydrate will often correct this, but it is sometimes necessary to mix a tablespoon of All-Bran with the meat to give bulk.

Supplements are needed by the puppy to grow strong teeth and straight bones. Many proprietary brands containing calcium, phosphorus and vitamins A and D are available, but the one that I have found suits Collies best is Ossivite capsules. Most puppies will eat them like sweets or swallow them with food. Give two daily to start with, increasing to five or six a day at eight months, then decreasing and discontinuing when the dog is a year old.

Water should be freely available but Collie puppies are

Sally Anne Thompson

likely to paddle in their water bowl; until this phase is over put only a small quantity of water down at a time in as heavy a dish as possible on a tray or layers of newspaper.

Never feed cooked bones of any sort to your dog. A large raw marrow bone once a week will be popular with both a puppy or an adult and will help to keep the teeth in good condition.

*Looking after the Puppy*
Just as important as a nourishing diet, the puppy must have adequate rest and sleep, so sleeping quarters must be arranged before you collect him. Decide where you want him to sleep, not forgetting that at eight weeks old he won't be house-trained. Most people choose the kitchen, but a conservatory, sun room or enclosed porch are all equally suitable unless the dog is to sleep out of doors in a kennel with a run. Make a bed for the puppy (an old wooden drawer is excellent, or a strong cardboard box with the front cut down). Line the bed with plenty of newspapers and then put in a piece of old blanket or an old wool jersey. It is a waste of money to buy a wicker dog basket for a puppy as he will chew it up, and discard it as an adult as being uncomfortable. Collies prefer to lie stretched out on their side and rarely curl up. As the puppy grows,

the box can be discarded and a heavy blanket, folded up, or an old rug, especially one with a rubber backing, can act as a bed.

When you bring your puppy home, let him wander round the room where he is going to sleep so he knows the surroundings. Let him play about a bit but do not overexcite him or introduce him to too many strange things at once. Give him a meal according to the time of day and when he has finished put him in the garden or on a sheet of newspaper to be clean. He'll want to be clean after he has been fed and immediately on waking, and if you praise him when he is clean in the right place (showing mild disapproval if he makes a puddle indoors) he will quickly learn to be clean during the day, though he may need a newspaper for the night. Most puppies give warning; some whine or bark, others stand by the door, or pant or wander about restlessly.

A word of warning: puppies can wriggle through the tiniest gap in a fence or hedge, or under the gate, so for the first few days stay with him in the garden to make sure he hasn't found an 'un-dog-proof' way out. It is easier to fence off a small section of garden close to the house where you can put him and be certain he can't disappear when your back is turned for a moment.

When you have introduced your puppy to his new home and fed him and he shows signs of sleepiness, put him in his bed and encourage him to stay there. Use the same word each time you put him in: 'Bed' is probably easiest; after a few days he will know to go to bed on command. Regular rest is essential to a growing puppy and he should sleep for a couple of hours each morning and afternoon; if there are children in the family they must learn not to disturb the puppy while he's resting.

When you first get your puppy he will have to be vaccinated against the five major diseases dogs can get: hard pad, distemper, hepatitis and two sorts of kidney disease. Your vet will advise on the best vaccine and give the first injection at about nine weeks. The second permanent one cannot be given until the puppy is more than twelve weeks old. Until he has been vaccinated and protection has been allowed to build up your puppy must be kept away from other dogs and places where they are. At three and a half months your puppy should be safe to go out on streets, parks and commons.

While the puppy will get enough exercise running about in the house and garden, it is a good plan to start his education for the time when he'll be able to go out. If you intend to take him in the car regularly, the earlier he gets used to it the better. Even before vaccination is complete, take him out for short journeys, giving him confidence by allowing him to sit next to you. Most Collies enjoy car travel, but if he suffers from travel sickness the best remedy I have found is Sea Legs. Give one (or two tablets if he is a very bad traveller) the night before or a couple of hours before setting off. Avoid heavy meals immediately before the journey, and exercise before starting. After a few trips the puppy will overcome the problem and no longer need treatment.

Please remember that dogs in cars need more air than we do. It is extremely cruel to leave a dog in a car with no ventilation and in summer he should only be left for a very short time. There are excellent ventilators that can be fitted to a car window in seconds which allow the window to be open but prevent the dog getting out (or anybody else getting in).

The puppy can be trained at home to walk on a lead. Some Collies can be difficult about this; they follow and walk to heel happily but consider a lead an unnecessary indignity. Use guile and persuasion. Buy a light leather or nylon puppy collar and leave it on the puppy all the time until he forgets about it. Attach a light lead or length of cord to the collar and let it trail along after the puppy while he follows you about. Take hold of the lead gently when the opportunity arises and let him trot along. Do not apply any tension. Until he discovers the trick all will be well, but he may stage a sit-down strike if he feels restrained. If you wait he'll probably get bored and start off again, otherwise you can tempt him with a morsel of food. After a few trial runs, with much praise when he walks properly on a lead, you will be able to go out into the big

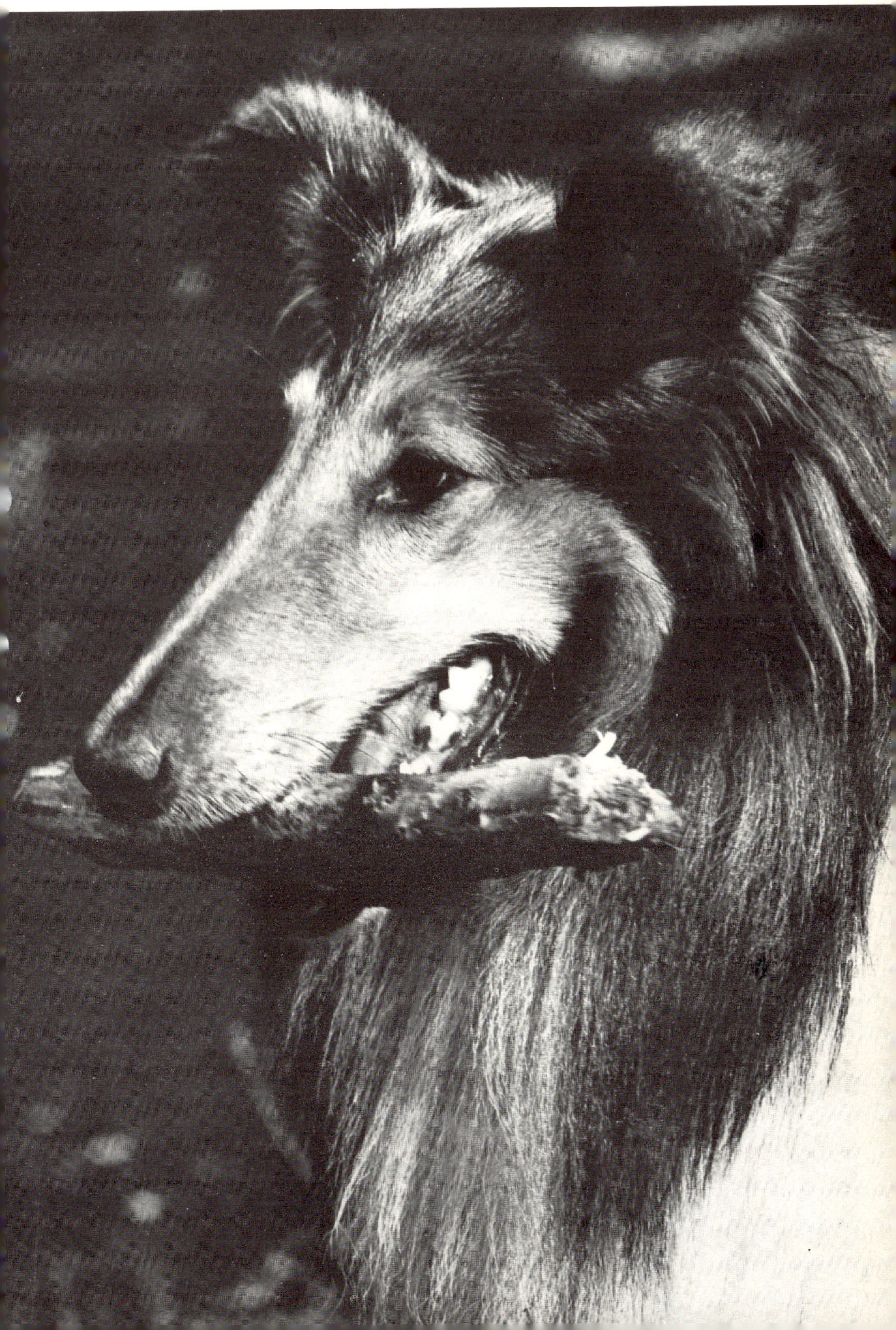

wide world when the vet gives the all clear.

The worst collar for the Collie is a metal choke chain as it ruins the neck hair; a nylon or leather choke collar should be just as good. All my adult dogs wear collars permanently, even the show dogs. These are very light rolled leather collars with a very narrow strap and buckle for minimum contact with the coat. Each one has an identification disc should the dog get lost. I remove the collar for the weekly grooming session and find that continually taking off and putting on the collar seems to damage the hair more. Collies are just the right height to be held by the collar (if necessary) but an adult will require a light lead only for exercise. Younger dogs are safer on a nylon or leather choke collar and lead since because the Collie has a rather thin head on a muscular neck it is fairly easy to slip out of a normal collar.

*Exercise*
Collies do not demand a great deal of exercise; left to themselves they are very lazy, preferring for example to run back to a gap in the hedge rather than jumping the gate. Although they are quite capable of jumping six feet or more they can be confined with no trouble by a fence only four feet high. They especially enjoy running free in a field or park, so try to arrange a period each day. Start with a brisk walk of ten to fifteen minutes followed by hard exercise in an open space where the dog can be let off the lead. Collies enjoy fetching sticks thrown for them (some will fetch a ball but this can be dangerous as a Collie can quite easily swallow an ordinary sized dog ball). End the session with another short brisk walk. This should provide you and your Collie with enough exercise to keep you both fit and well. Your puppy will naturally have to work up gradually to this full routine as he should never get over-tired.

Many adult Collies are reluctant to be clean in their own garden, so may need an extra five-minute walk morning and night; please respect other people's property and do not allow him to foul the pavement or other people's gardens or driveways – make sure he uses the gutter or waste ground.

Most Collies are good at coming when called, even when they are enjoying themselves, but as adolescents they often experiment by becoming temporarily deaf to all commands. If this happens when you are exercising your Collie do not shout after him or give chase – give a sharp whistle, turn and walk in the opposite direction. This takes courage but it usually works, as nothing upsets a Collie more than being ignored. Your apparent lack of concern will bring him running back to you, when you can praise him before putting him back on the lead. This phase should soon pass, but if your Collie is particularly difficult at coming back the best plan is not to let him off the lead for several days. Take him to the usual favourite places, but insist he walks to heel all the time, praising him for doing so. After a few walks like this, let him off the lead but do not let him go too far before calling him back and praising him before he runs off again.

When it comes to giving your Collie some basic training, remember that the breed is rather sensitive and does not take kindly to bullying, nagging or force of any kind. Be firm, give your commands authoritatively and above all never lose your temper.

Basically the Collie wants to serve and please, but he will not grovel and rarely asks a favour. In return he seeks your companionship, preferably for twenty-four hours a day. Collies are very expressive dogs, and as well as 'talking' – a peculiar sing-song whine reserved for special people, usually one or two members of the family – they show their feelings by the carriage and position of the ears and various tail movements. It will not take a new owner long to interpret these signs; alert ears, a laughing expression and high tail carriage means a happy Collie anticipating a walk or a game, tucked up tail and clipped back ears means an apprehensive Collie, flattened ears and screwed up eyes, with tail tip tentatively wagging means an apologetic Collie, and so on. The pleasure of owning a Collie will grow as understanding develops.

One point to watch is that Collies are very tough and do not make a fuss if unwell or hurt, making every effort to carry on normally. If your Collie goes off his food, is unusually quiet, if the ears twitch continually, indicating pain, or if they are continually held back tight to the sides of the head and the eyes have a dull or worried look, be on the safe side and consult the veterinary surgeon as soon as possible.

If your Collie, who normally has a stable temperament, becomes edgy and nervous, and seems frightened of hitherto commonplace things, it is likely to be due to a deficiency of Vitamin B (the breed seems to require more than other breeds). If the symptoms appear, Benerva compound tablets, obtainable from the chemist, contain all the B group vitamins; most dogs will eat them like sweets but they can be mixed with the meat meal if necessary. Give six to eight tablets daily for ten days, then four daily for another two weeks. This course can be repeated at intervals if necessary, but any dog showing a need for extra B vitamins should be kept on a daily dose of Brewer's Yeast tablets or Bemax. It is beneficial for these, and all dogs, to add about four ounces of chopped raw liver once a week; liver acts as a tonic and contains many essential nutrients. Cooked liver will nearly always produce very loose bowel actions and should not be fed in any quantity.

*Grooming*
A healthily fed and exercised Collie, to do it credit, should also be well groomed to get the admiration he deserves.

As a puppy, a Collie will look and feel like a cuddly teddy bear with a very short thick coat, showing a 'halo' of long hair round the neck and along the back. At this stage, apart from keeping the coat clean and free of parasites, very little serious grooming is necessary. The puppy should *never* be bathed except on the vet's advice. A clean bed and fresh bedding should ensure a clean dog, but if persistent dust baths or visits to the coal cellar make a wash and brush up essential, the following treatment is effective. Add a tablespoon of Dettol to a bowl of warm water, wring out a flannel in the solution and rub the puppy vigorously with it until he is slightly damp all over. Towel him dry and brush out against the lie of the coat (from the tail to the head) until he is absolutely dry. Collies do not usually have skin problems, but the coat must be kept free from fleas and lice that might make the dog scratch and cause a break in the skin. There are many excellent preparations available and, for a coat like the Collie's, aerosol sprays are easiest to use and most effective, though they are more expensive than powders. Some Collies are troubled with scurvy coats that make the dog itch and scratch even when free from parasites. This condition is usually due to a lack of fat in the diet, as heavy-coated dogs need a certain amount to keep the coat in good condition. The addition of a teaspoon of corn oil or a little chopped suet sprinkled on the food daily should improve the condition. A slight mineral deficiency will aggravate a scurvy coat, and a dessertspoon of Complan sprinkled on the food daily will supply any trace elements lacking in the diet.

From the outset, get the puppy used to being brushed, and encourage him to stand still while it is being done. Use a good quality bristle or nylon hairbrush with the tufts set in a rubber cushion and always keep it scrupulously clean. There is no need to comb out a young puppy but at four or four and a half months the new coat begins to show through the puppy fluff, usually as a dark streak running down the centre of the back. When this happens it is essential to begin removing the dead puppy coat. A fairly wide-toothed comb is the most useful and easiest to manage, and a little daily combing, in addition to brushing, will help to remove the puppy fluff. By about six months the teddy bear coat will have changed to a short, dense, shining jacket of straight, hardish texture and the leg and tail featherings will have begun to appear. This is the time to establish a regular grooming routine.

Bear in mind that a coat has to be *grown*, and that no amount of grooming will produce one if the dog is not kept in peak condition. A balanced diet, plenty of fresh air and exercise and, above all, companionship and an interest in life giving mental and physical well-being will be reflected in a gleaming well-conditioned coat.

Given a good coat to groom, here is the basic procedure (which applies to both the show dog and the pet). Have a short daily tidy up and one main session a week of intensive grooming. Daily grooming is best done after the main exercise period; allow the dog a short rest and time for a drink, then give a quick vigorous brush through the coat to remove any bits of twig or bramble and smarten the coat up. This will take only three to four minutes.

The weekly grooming should be done on the same day each week; it will take about half an hour. You will need the dog in one place for the whole session, so it is a good idea to get him used to being tied on to a heavy piece of furniture or post – most dogs get bored after a while and will wander off if given the opportunity. Start by vigorously brushing the coat, starting at the tail end and working towards the head. Wring out a flannel or towel in Dettol solution (see page ▲) and rub it all over the coat, paying particular attention to the underside of the chest and between the legs. Don't forget the face; rub it gently with the flannel, carefully avoiding the eyes. Do not soak the coat but dampen it slightly all over then rub dry with a rough towel. Finish off with another good brush until each hair gives the impression of being separate. Comb the leg and tail featherings and the long hair at the base of the ears, but don't comb the body coat unless the dog is moulting. Over-zealous use of the comb will break the top coat and loosen the undercoat, preventing the dog from growing a true Collie coat. Some dogs grow a fuzz of soft hair at the base of the ears which has a tendency to matt and form quite hard balls of fur; if this happens cut the matt out carefully and try to keep the ears free by removing further growths of hair. Rub a chalk block over the hair and pull it out by grasping a few hairs at a time between the thumb and forefinger. A little practice makes this an easy procedure and does not hurt the dog as the hair is dead.

Collies do not need trimming in the way a terrier or poodle does, but the removal of surplus hair on the feet and legs not only make the dog look better; in bad weather he will bring in less mud and wet and be easier to dry. This trimming needs to be done about once a month with a pair of sharp round-bladed scissors. Trim out all the hair between the pads on each foot, then trim the outside edges of the pads, following the natural shape of the foot. With the dog standing, remove any long hair that stands up between the pads on the top of the foot, taking off a little at a time (do not over-trim, just make the feet look neat, tidy and natural). On the hind legs, from the point of the hock where the long featherings end to the ground, the hair often grows raggedly. Comb this hair out away from the bone and cut it in a straight line about an inch from the bone with long-bladed scissors, starting at the heel. Comb the remaining hair down to give a smooth appearance.

As you groom your dog each week, give him a physical check over. Feel the body, which should be hard and firm. The bones should be covered but there should not be any surplus rolls of flesh; make a note to adjust the diet if the dog appears to be over- or under-weight. It is a good plan to weigh him regularly, carrying him on the bathroom scales and deducting your own weight. Check the condition of the coat and skin and treat for parasitic infections if signs are seen. Look for the first signs of any skin lesions and seek advice if these are found. Examine the mouth and teeth. Excessive tartar or bleeding or soreness of the gums should be treated by the vet. Examine the ears and make sure they are clean and do not have an offensive smell. Although Collies rarely get ear infections, they sometimes accumulate dirt and grease around the ear opening which can be wiped clean with damp cotton-wool; do not poke or probe into the ear itself as damage can easily be done. The nose should be moist, clean and black and any discharge should be considered abnormal. However, Collies that are elderly or like digging holes often get a cracked sore-looking nose which can be treated with a little Vaseline.

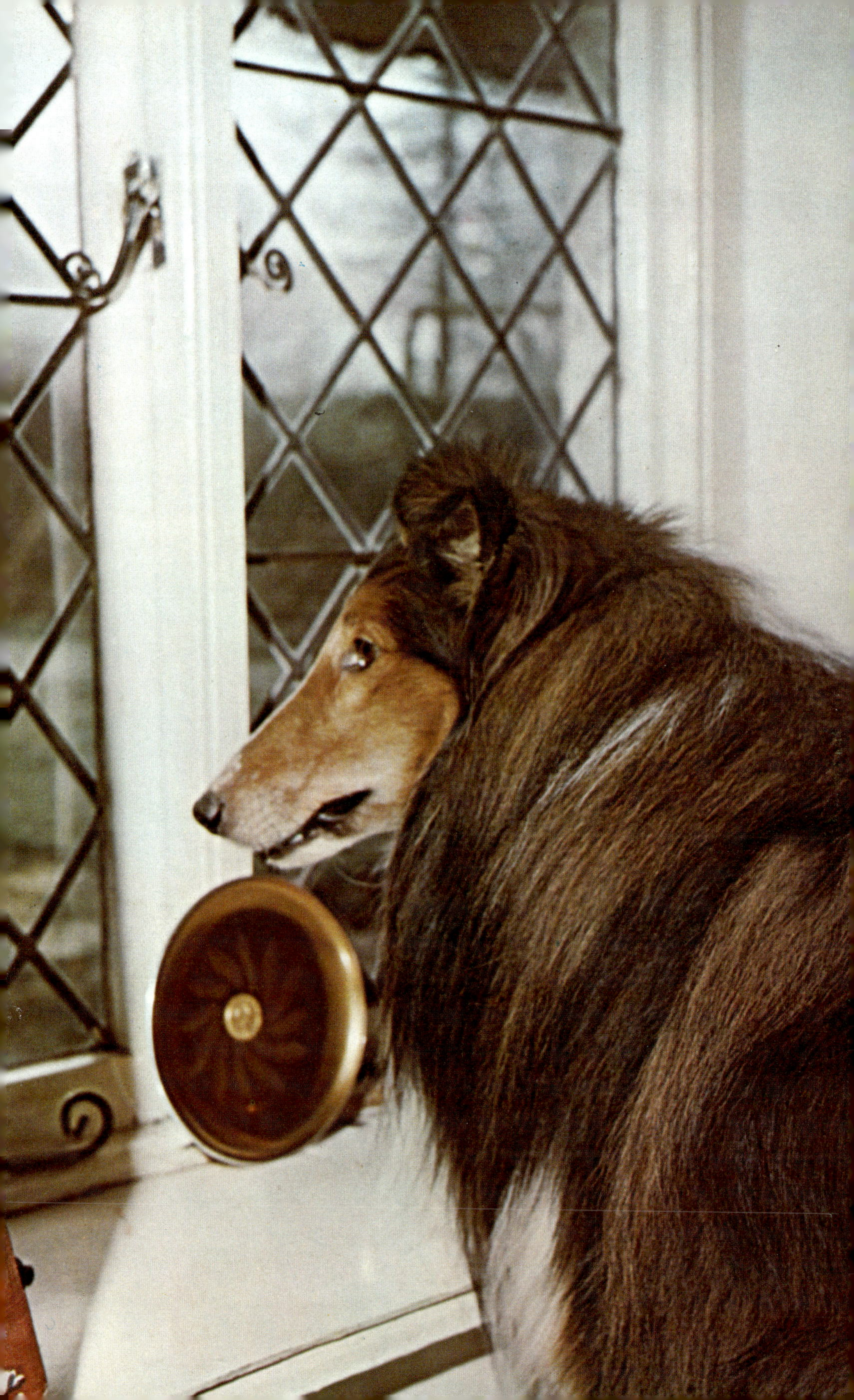

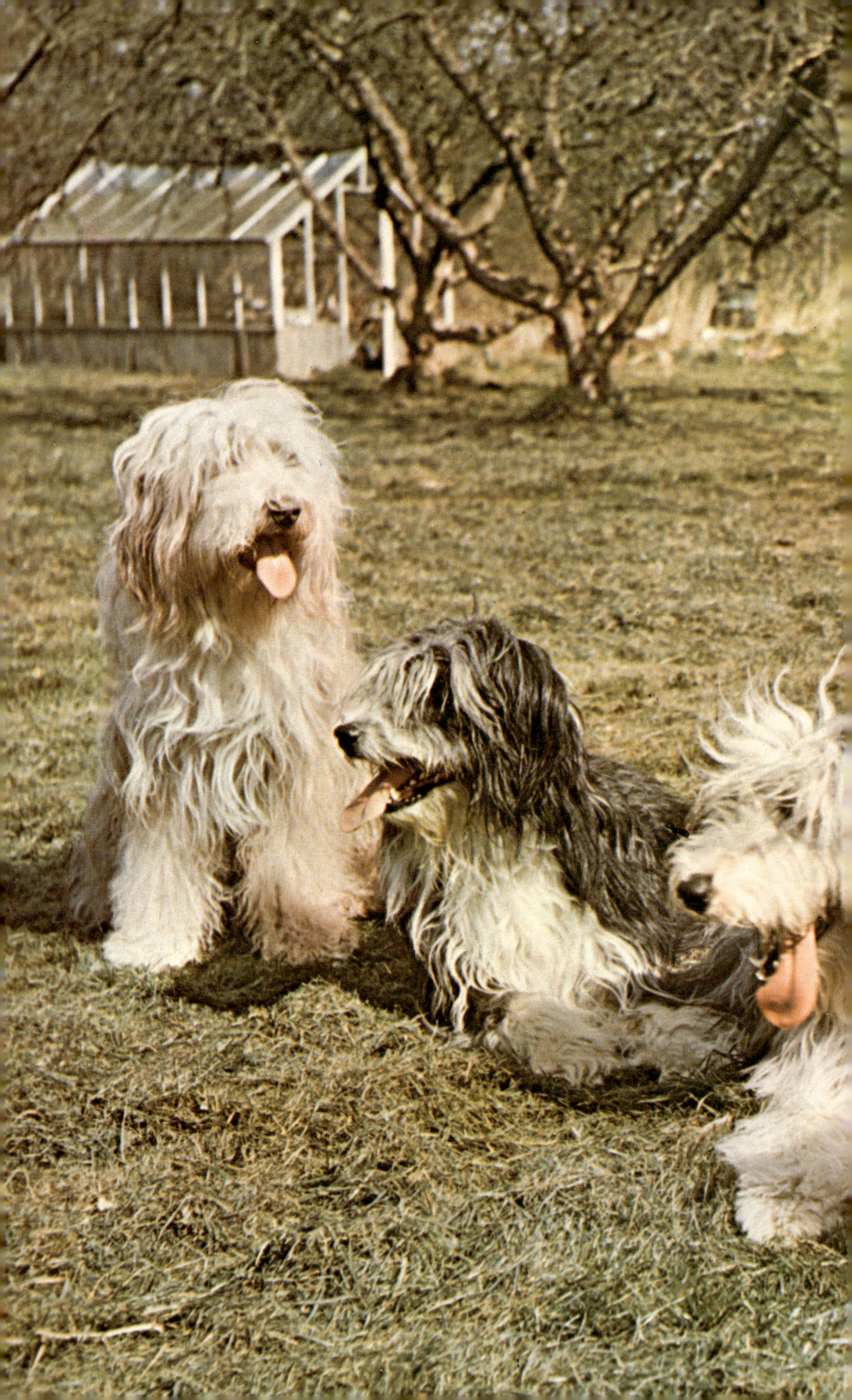

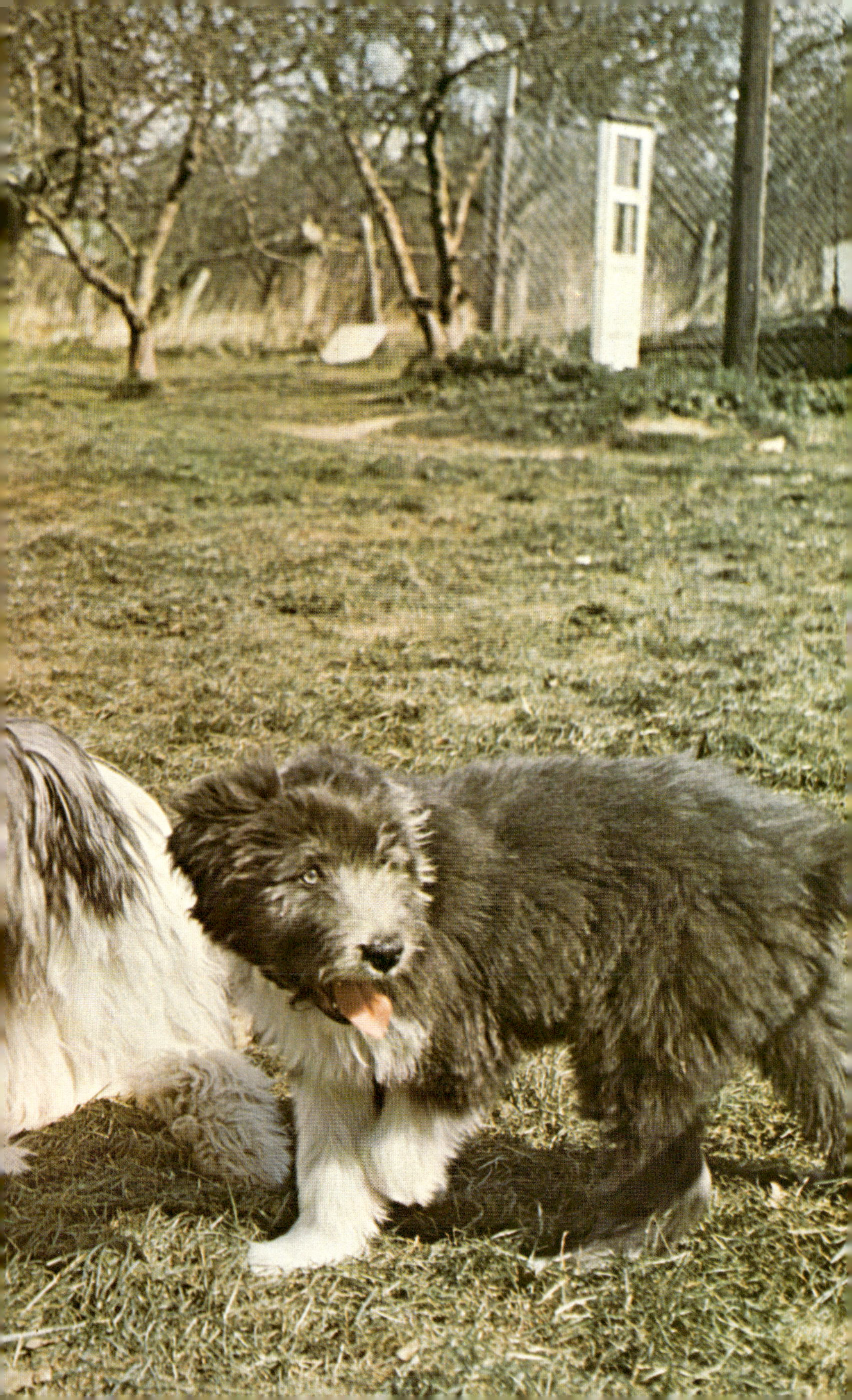

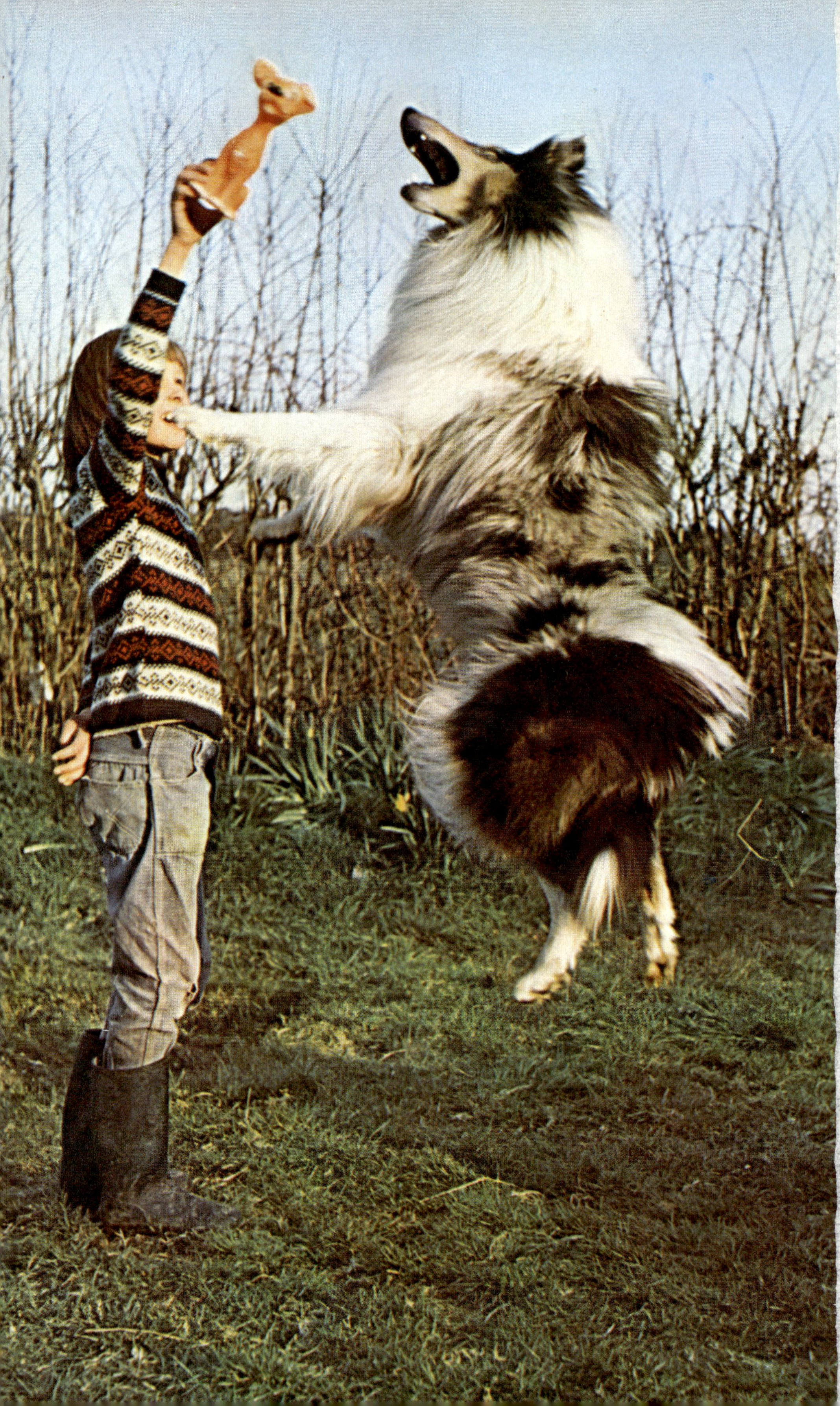

The eyes cause the most trouble. As they are deep set, the corner cavities often collect dirt and grit. It is important to keep the eyes free from all foreign matter, which can be wiped out with cotton-wool soaked in cold boiled water. If an eye runs continually or shows signs of redness or infection, get professional advice as soon as possible. Antibiotic eye ointments will clear up eye infections quickly, and an application once a week will prevent infection recurring. If the infected eye is neglected too long, the tear duct will become permanently blocked, making the dog's eyes water permanently and look unsightly. During teething and cold windy weather, normal eyes may water, but this will quickly cease.

Examine the feet, making sure there are no cuts on the pads and that the skin between the pads is not inflamed or raw. If they are caked with mud and dirt, wash the feet and dry them thoroughly, dusting with a little talcum powder.

*Moulting*
This is probably the biggest problem facing a Collie owner, and the coat needs different treatment. As I said before, after the baby coat has been shed, the Collie grows his first adult coat which is often heavier and slightly more wavy and soft in texture than the true adult coat. This coat is usually cast between eleven and fourteen months old (a little later for a bitch). For the male, it is probably the most drastic moult he will have, but a bitch, after having puppies, will cast even more completely. The soft undercoat is the first to be shed; it starts by lifting away from the skin and can be combed out with a wide-toothed metal comb – comb daily until it has all been cast. Then the top coat will drop out; again, comb this out daily. Although I do not usually advocate bathing a Collie at this time, it can be a great help in hastening the removal of dead hair. Use a reliable brand of dog shampoo and tepid water, rinsing well afterwards (if you use the family bath remember to put something over the plug hole or the plumbing will get blocked with hairs). The sooner the old coat is removed the quicker the new coat will grow.

Growth can be encouraged by a daily brushing with a damp brush, dipping the brush into a bowl of water and shaking out the excess. Rain water is particularly effective.

After this first moult the male Collie may take some time to grow an adult coat and may even have a second moult at about two. From the age of three he will have grown the heavy coat with the typical long mane associated with the male of the breed, and from then on will look the same almost all the year round, losing a bit of undercoat from time to time and growing it again simultaneously.

The bitch moults differently; as a rule, bitches start to drop coat two or three months after being in season. As they get older and season less frequently, coat casting decreases as well. Like the dog, the first moult is often the worst although they do not lose as much top coat as the male. However, should the bitch have a litter of puppies, the coat fall afterwards will be so severe that it may cause concern. When the puppies are about three months old the poor mother will look almost naked with a tail like a piece of old string; but the new coat soon grows and by the time the puppies are six months old she will have grown a brand new gleaming jacket.

After exercise in bad weather you may be faced with the problem of an apparently soaking wet bedraggled dog – don't despair. Before bringing him into the house encourage him to shake to get rid of most of the surplus (usually over you if you're not careful). If the dog won't co-operate and shake by himself, tickle the inside of his ear gently and this should encourage him. Sit the dog on a thick pile of newspaper in the corner of the kitchen and leave him while you deal with your personal comfort. When you return you will find that most of the dirt and wet have transferred themselves from the dog to the newspaper and he can be rubbed down with a towel. A quick brush through will restore him to normal; although he may be slightly damp on top he will be quite dry underneath.

Any hairs on carpets or upholstery can be removed with a damp sponge-mop, and the sticky side of adhesive tape quickly deals with hairs on dark dresses or suits.

*Ears*
No Collie book would be complete without a mention of the breed's pet bogey – ears. The dogs on cards and chocolate boxes are all too frequently depicted with erect ears like an Alsatian and many people think this is correct. A Collie should have the top third of the ear tipped over so that it is carried in a semi-erect position. This correct ear carriage is essential to obtain the characteristically attractive face of the breed. Prick ears are not so common now because most of our breeding stock now has natural ear carriage. Although ears can be 'helped' into the correct position, a puppy born with pricked ears will always have them, no matter how much time and trouble is put into trying to make them tip over. A puppy should have heavy floppy ears which gradually come up, and may well be carried in the correct position for a few weeks when he is from ten to sixteen weeks old. The trouble usually starts at teething time at about four and a half months old. I like to see a puppy of this age completely 'flop' his ears, for he will end up with correctly carried ears with no assistance from

anyone. Some puppies will begin to 'throw' their ears at teething time; one day one ear will be pricked and the next days it will be floppy and the other pricked. These puppies also generally end up with good natural ear carriage, although they may need a little help and attention.

The puppies that cause the most bother are the ones that suddenly shoot both ears skywards with no hint of a droop. Some pet owners do not have strong feelings about the way their Collie carries his ears, but for those who would prefer him to carry his ears correctly, here are a few hints. If an ear stays erect for more than forty-eight hours, treat it in the following manner. Buy a small tin of Kaolin Poultice from the chemist, stir the contents (but do not heat) and apply a little to the inside third of the ear. Dip the treated ear in bird sand, ash or garden soil to absorb the stickiness and add weight. The poultice will harden and drop off; after a few weeks, you may find that the dressing has dropped off completely and the ears are carried perfectly. Some ears may need new applications of Kaolin Poultice until teething is complete at about nine months. Bitches sometimes prick their ears before and during a season, and their ears should be treated in the same way. If by the time your Collie is a year old his ears are still pricked in spite of treatment, I'm afraid there is nothing to be done. If the sight of a prick-eared Collie offends you (as it does me) you can cheat by sticking a piece of chewing gum on the tip of each ear which will transform the look of the ears immediately. The gum stays in place for weeks, causes no discomfort to the dog and is quite unnoticeable.

**AILEEN SPEDING**
Mrs Speding worked for seventeen years in a busy London small-animal veterinary practice as an assistant and gained in this time considerable experience in operating and X-raying. She bought her first pedigree dog, a Shetland Sheepdog, in 1948 and her first Collie in 1951, breeding her first litter in 1953.
In the same year she registered the now world famous Collie and Sheltie prefix 'Antoc'. She won her first challenge certificate in 1956 and since then has won over forty with Collies and Shelties, one of the most famous being the Collie champion Antoc Vicar

of Bray. This is a wonderful record when one considers that Mrs Speding never keeps more than eight adults and breeds on average only one or two litters a year. She first judged in 1956, and her first championship judging appointment was with Rough Collies. She has judged both Shelties and Collies at Cruft's and many other important shows in Britain and on the Continent. Mrs Speding has exported winning champions to Finland, Sweden, Norway, Italy, Australia, Rhodesia, New Zealand, Denmark and Israel. At one time she was secretary of both the London Collie Club and the London and Provincial Collie Club. She served on the committee of the Bournemouth Championship Show, but resigned when she became secretary of the Collie Association. She is also a permanent delegate to the Rough Collie Breed Council.

# 2 The Rough Collie
BY MARGARET OSBORNE

The Pastoral breeds, world wide, form one of the most important groups. I do not write this sentence with the show ring in mind, but with the idea that, without the *canis familiaris palustris* Man himself might never have emerged from his wild state, and might even never have survived. Toussenel, the Frenchman, wrote: 'It is thanks to the dog that mankind emerged from his wild state, for he gave him the herds of cattle. Without the dog, no herds or flocks, without these latter, no assured subsistence'.

Undoubtedly dogs and reindeer were the first animals to be domesticated by man, although such are the mists of antiquity that no one can say at what epoch this domestication occurred. However, we are certain that it happened an extremely long time ago and certainly as early as the Stone Age.

In different areas of the world the sheep-dog takes different shapes to adapt itself to the terrain in which it has to work and live. Even in the same country there may be different types of sheep-dog in different areas; for instance, the little Shetland Sheepdog lives in the islands in the far north, and its larger close relation the Collie elsewhere. The method by which the different types of sheep-dog work may also be quite clearly defined.

In the early days no thought was ever given to the beauty of the animal; it was bred for work, and work alone, so it is not wrong to say that the early selection programme was always one for natural ability and working qualities, plus, undoubtedly, health and stamina. He was bred as helper and servant only.

Dog shows were non-existent prior to the 1860s, so no standard existed for any breed, and although we find descriptions of dogs over two thousand years old, and minute descriptions at that, nowhere can we find any documentation which could possibly apply to our Collie until well into the nineteenth century.

In its earliest days of domestication, the dog would have been used mainly to guard its master from the attacks of wild beasts, and certainly also as an animal of prey, helping to fill the stockpot. It cannot have been long before some of these dogs emerged not just as guardians of the herds of reindeer, but as workers of these herds also, and from them would have emerged the perhaps more gentle type of worker which in time became the sheep-dog – a dog which was willing to accept the will of man. When, one may ask, did dog become the guardian of the flocks, the helper of the nomadic shepherd, and finally the constant companion and assistant of the man who had established his flocks, his family and himself, in his own particular area?

Almost certainly the sheep-dog can be traced back to Roman times, or even earlier, and in the Old Testament we read of sheep-dogs tending the flocks (Job XXX, 1).

At the time of the Roman invasion of Britain, the sheep-dog was almost certainly introduced from farther east, for all armies had their dogs travelling with them, and some would be left behind from time to time when the invaders returned home – or if not the actual dogs themselves, undoubtedly their offspring.

The Collie, as a show animal, begins his story just about

the same time as did dog shows themselves. The first ever dog show was held in Newcastle in June 1859, with another in Birmingham in November of the same year, but these two were confined to sporting dogs only. In December of 1860 the first show to include a class for sheep-dogs was held, which meant, of course, that the Collies, if any were shown at all, were lumped together with the Bobtails, the herder's dog, and any other type which might reasonably be included in this grouping. No information remains of the winner, except that it was 'Mr Wakefield's bitch'. The unanswered question is, 'Was she a Collie?' In those days registration was not compulsory, the Kennel Club was not yet in being, and even when the first issue of the Kennel Club Stud Book appeared it contained numerous entries for dogs which had no details at all. It was very unhelpful in lots of other ways too, because we get as the results of the Manchester Show in 1867:

*Sheep-dogs: 1st Palethorpe's Rover, 2nd Percival's Rover, 3rd Horsepool's Rover.*

From the early show records which we have it appears that the sheep-dog classes were very popular, almost every show scheduling them. Quite early on the same owners' names begin to appear and reappear, and one of the very early enthusiasts was a Mr J. Siviter. His first win was at Birmingham in 1861 (though this does not appear in the Stud Book) and is described in the show awards as Jeho (Scotch dog) and nothing more. But as much as twenty-five years later this early die-hard was still exhibiting.

Stud Book entries varied between Colleys, Collies and Sheep-dogs over a number of years, presumably according to the whims of the Kennel Club. But quite early on they were sub-divided into 'Rough-coated, Smooth-coated, Short-tailed'. The latter achieved its own classification in the Stud Book rather earlier than did our breed, for it was not until the volume was published in 1895 that the dogs became known as Collies (Rough) and Collies (Smooth). Today, of course, we have Rough Collies and Smooth Collies – two different breeds, no longer varieties of the same breed.

However, even before the breed settled into its proper

classification, some of the dogs to which Collies throughout the world owe so much had begun to make their mark. Mr S. E. Shirley, founder of the Kennel Club, played a large part also in the making of the Collie as a show dog, for he was breeder and owner of the great Trefoil, and it is to this dog that every Collie, of either coat and either sex world wide can trace his ancestry in direct tail-male.

At Birmingham in 1871 two more dogs whose names became household words in their breed, made their debut, Old Mec and Old Cockie. On this occasion they were placed first and second in that order. In the opinion of those who saw them, Old Cockie was by far the better of the two great dogs, and he certainly played a much larger part in the improvement of the breed, and also dominated the show ring for the next three years. It is sad that we have no knowledge of the antecedents of either of these great pillars of the breed.

By 1875, when the Birmingham entry had crept up from seventeen four years before to sixty-two names, both human and canine, began to fill the records – names to be conjured with, names which still live in memory today. Trefoil was just beginning his career, together with his son Scott. The Charles brothers, of the Wellesbourne Kennel, were first noted, and what pictures of the greats of the past that word 'Wellesbourne' evokes. Ch. Charlemagne and his owner and breeder Mr J. Bissell made their first appearance in 1877. The following year the grand old man, the Rev Hans Hamilton made his first foray, this time without success, for his Trefoil II was unplaced, but when he purchased this dog from the Hon Everard Digby, he also acquired Captain and two bitches Eva and Ruby, the latter two daughters of Nellie, from whom some fifty per cent of today's challenge certificate winners are descended. The prefix Woodmansterne speedily became one to be held in awe.

Mr A. H. Megson came on the scene in 1882. He was in a position to be able to pay record prices for his dogs, and almost every top class dog of its day was in his ownership for some part of its life. He owned, amongst others, Ch. Rutland, Ch. Metchley Wonder, Ch. Caractacus, Ch. Edgbaston Fox, Ch. Southport Perfection, Ch. Ormskirk Emerald, for which he paid Mr Tom Stretch the unheard of price of £1,500, at that time an enormous amount.

Tom Stretch entered the arena three years after Mr Megson, but very quickly established the Ormskirks in a near unassailable position. It was in this year too (1885) that the blue merle first made its mark in history. This year for the very first time two merles, Mr Arkwright's Ch. Blue Ruin and Ch. Blue Sky were able to hold the other colours at bay.

In 1886 Mr Hugo Ainscough and his Parbolds came into the game, the greatest of these being Ch. Parbold Piccolo, who had a great influence on the breed, and in 1889 Mr

H. E. Packwood came along with the Billesleys, especially renowned for the lovely blue merles they produced. One year later came Mr W. E. Mason and the Southports.

Eight years went by before Mr R. H. Lord put the Seedleys on the scene, and they made a great impact.

After this it was not until just before the first war that Mr W. Stansfield and his Launds were launched (this prefix is being carried on today by his daughter Mrs Bishop). His name, and the name of the Launds will never be erased as long as the breed exists. What a red letter year this was, for then also were the Edens of Mr F. Robson born. Too soon, alas, came the war and it was almost ten years before dogs could take their proper part in the lives of their owners again, for in 1917 the Kennel Club banned the breeding of dogs, except under licence, and this ban held for two years.

This seems an appropriate spot to terminate this history of the breed, for what has happened in the last five decades is not really history; most of it is still with us, and the records there for all to see.

## MARGARET OSBORNE

Miss Margaret Osborne, owner of the well-known 'Shiel' prefix, is one of the strongest personalities in the modern dog world with a lifetime spent in most branches of pedigree dogs. Miss Osborne showed her first dog, a Shetland Sheepdog, when still at school, and started breeding Collies seriously when she lived in Australia in the early 40s. Before the war Miss Osborne concentrated solely on obedience work, and in particular working trials, and was the first person to own and train a breed other than an Alsatian to win a working trial challenge certificate. For a number of years she has been in great demand both in Britain and abroad as a judge of all breeds. She has judged in every Continent, and I would imagine has judged abroad more than any other Collie specialist. This year (1973) Miss Osborne judged the working group at Cruft's and she is planning her fifth judging trip to the United States. Author of five dog books, she has bred or owned champion Collies, Shetland Sheepdogs, Corgis and Dachshunds. Her latest acquisition is a fairly new breed to Britain, a French sheepdog called the Briard.

## 3 The Smooth Collie
BY JOAN E. HILL

It would appear that there are no written records about Collies, Rough or Smooth, before 1860. This does not mean that there were no such breeds as there is strong evidence that there were Collies of both coats in early Roman times and it is suggested that the Roman invaders brought their own breed of dog, probably a hunting type, and that these dogs bred with our own dogs here and evolved a working dog. The stone image of the Roman dog (see page ▲) found at Corbridge, Northumberland, does seem to support this idea.

During the sixteenth, seventeenth and eighteenth centuries, sheep raising had increased in the Highlands of Scotland, while in the Border counties and Northumberland cattle farming flourished. It was found that the smooth-coated variety was ideal as a cattle dog and that the rough-coated variety was better suited to the rigours of the colder climates in the Highlands. That the two varieties stem from one common ancestor is generally accepted, and it is clear from the early records that both coats frequently appeared in the same litter. It was by careful and selective breeding for coat that the two varieties were established.

There has always been much speculation about the origin of the name 'Collie'. It would appear that it is derived from the word 'Colley' which was given to a black-faced breed of sheep (Colig being Old English for coaly or black). In the early days breeders tried hard to breed an all-black, black and tan or any self-coloured dog – the absence of white was considered a great attribute in the early show Collies. One gets the same colours in Smooths as one gets in the Roughs, namely tri-colour, blue merle and sable or white, although the latter, for some reason, is not so popular with the older breeders today.

As it is widely known, the Smooth Collie has always been over-shadowed by his more glamorous brother, the Rough Collie, but the Smooth has great beauty too with his clean classical lines, uncluttered by coat, with nothing to conceal his faults nor mar his beauty. He appears to be

slightly smaller than the Rough, and it must be remembered that he is a working breed and that he must therefore be built on lines accordingly. If he has *over-long* legs or back, he cannot cover the ground in the required manner to work tirelessly. He must be muscular, strong but light of foot, his ears must be tipped to catch distant sounds and his eyes should be set slightly obliquely in his head so that he can see down the length of his nose to enable him to look a long way into the distance. His jacket must be short and dense with an abundance of undercoat to ensure it is weather-resistant, a deep spring of rib, plenty of heart room with well-muscled quarters, makes the Smooth Collie a true working dog.

That the Smooth has made progress during the last century no one will deny. In the very early show days the Smooth did not appeal to the dog fanciers as did the Rough. There were shows held in 1870 with classes for Smooths and at the Darlington shows there could usually be found a fairly reasonable collection of Smooths. In 1877 at the Birmingham dog show Mr Mapplebeck's Fan, a blue merle, won the class for Smooth Collies.

In January 1880 Mr F. Hurst of Knutsford bred a litter sired by a Rough dog out of a bitch named Snow. This litter produced the black and tan Ch. Pickmere, who later earned fame in the hands of Mr A. H. Megson.

Sally Anne Thompson

Sally Anne Thompson

Breeders by now were doing some very careful and selective breeding and many excellent Smooths were to be seen in the ring.

February 1900 saw the birth of what was probably the best Smooth to date, Ch. Babette of Morton, sired by Ch. Irthlingbro Village Boy ex Village Girl. Bred by Mr A. Dunmore she became the property of Mr H. Jones, on whose death she passed into the hands of that great Smooth Collie fancier Lady Alexander of Ballochmyle. That Babette was almost the perfect Smooth is without doubt and she could and did beat many of the top Roughs of that time. In 1902 at the Collie Club show she won the Challenge Trophy for the best Collie, Rough or Smooth. Babette was almost entirely Smooth bred.

Ch. Canute Perfection comes into the picture in 1903. Bred by Mr F. Farish, he was owned by Mr Wildgoose, whose Canutes were the most famous of all Smooths in that period. Later, this mating was repeated and the resulting litter produced a bitch who surpassed all before her, named Eleanor de Montford, who was owned by Mrs Munford-Smith.

At this stage there were many really good Smooths to be

seen and it is impossible for me to name them all.

Between the wars the Smooth Collie had its ups and downs. Many great dogs came and went; breeders such as Bart Hewison with his Hewburns; Gordon Foster, followed later by his son of the same name, with their Redevalleys; and Mr Stansfield and his Launds. It is to one of his dogs I dedicate this era: Ch. Laund Lynn, a superb blue merle bitch, the like of which is seldom seen.

After World War II, the Smooths emerged in a somewhat sorry state, but a few of the faithful fanciers got together and formed the Smooth Collie Club of Great Britain. These included Miss M. Osborne, the late Mr and Mrs H. Farrington with their Wythenshawes, the late Mr E. Allsop and Mrs Allsop of Wychelm fame, the Peterblue partners, Mrs Alexander and the late Miss Dundas Mouatt, Mrs Zoe Rhys and her Hughlys, Mrs Leslie, myself and others. We really did work hard to get the Smooth Collie back into the limelight. Of the dogs of this era, the Peterblue ladies had a great brood bitch, Ch. Redevalley Rosita of Ladypark. This bitch was the dam of many champions and challenge certificate winners, including my own Ch. Selskars Peterblue Susan, who has been likened by many to the illustrious Ch. Laund Lynn. Susan in her turn produced a line of consistent winners including many champions such as International Champion Selskars Thane, a blue merle dog who won his title in every country he was exhibited in. Ch. Selskars Soldanora, winner of fifteen challenge certificates owned by Mr and Mrs S. Saville; Mrs Jeanne Taylor's Ch. Crossfells Selskars Soldanella who became the second (if not the first) sable and white Smooth Collie champion in Great Britain.

Mr Farrington's tri-colour Ch. Wythenshawe Windhover must surely go down as one of the greats. He sired, to name only two, Mrs Nan Leach's beautiful blue merle champion Brystal of Rodlea, and my own dual challenge certificate winner Selskars Sabretta, who was the very first Smooth Collie ever to win the Junior Warrant. Ch. Windhover's dam was, in my opinion, one of the best Smooths I have ever seen. Wythenshawe Wattatreasure, she won three challenge certificates but as two were

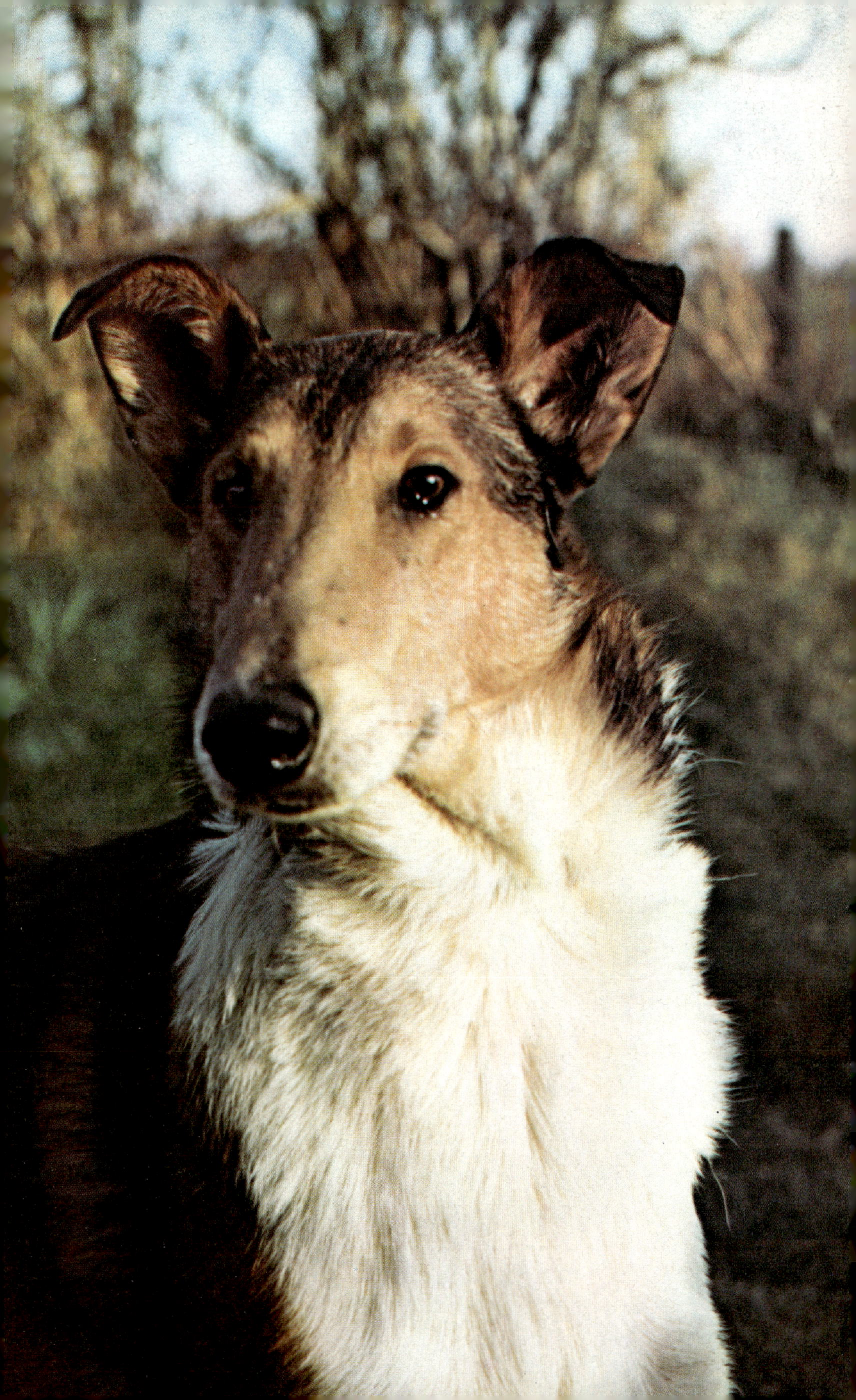

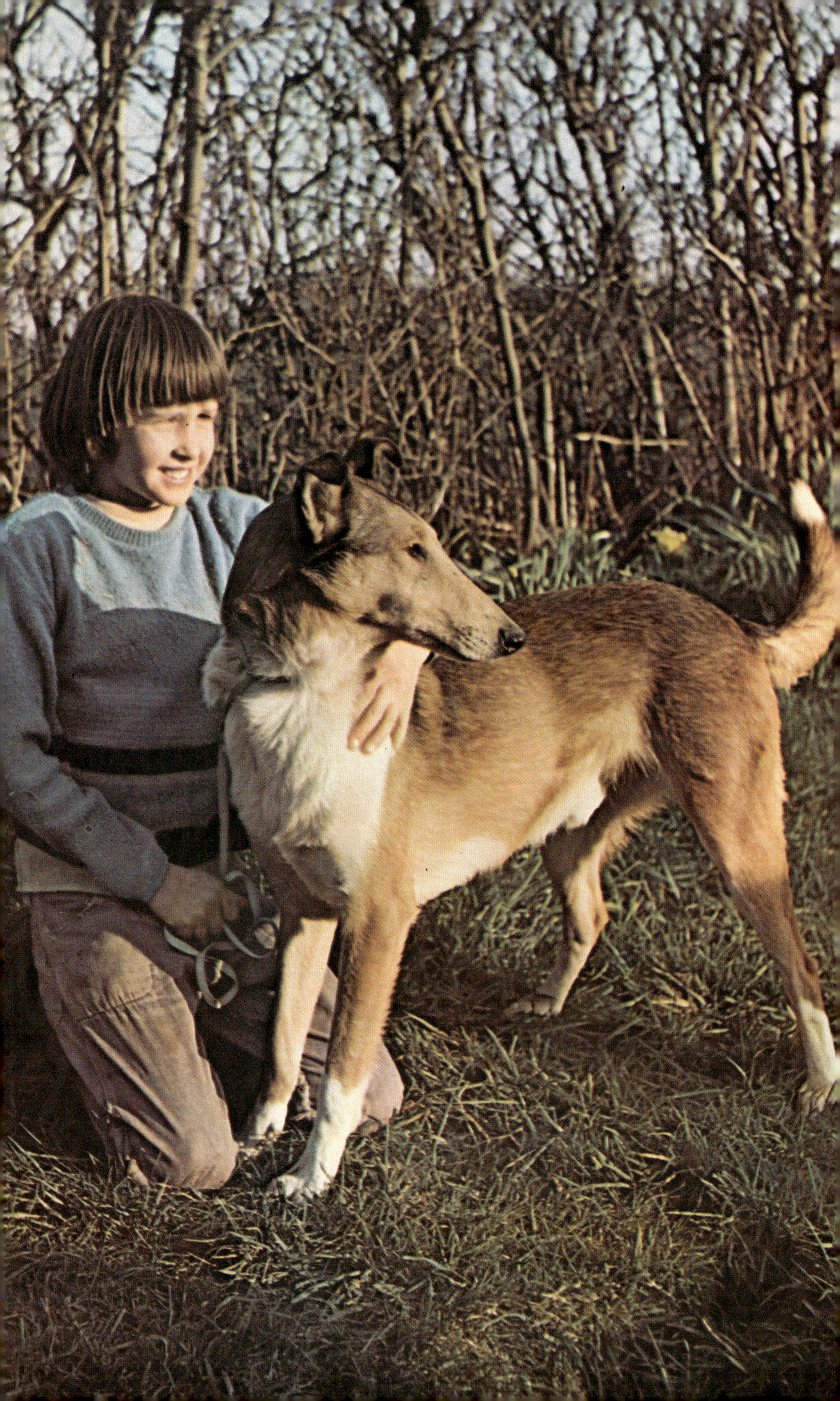

awarded by the same judge she did not get her title, due no doubt to the fact that she must have been about six years old when challenge certificates were granted to Smooths again.

From the Peterblue kennels came many champions, such as Ch. Peterblue Patricia and Ch. Peterblue Philippa. Peterblue Martie, who never did get her title, was, in my opinion, the best that this partnership ever showed.

Mrs Rhys's two blue merle champion dogs, Hughly Hushpuppy Blue and Hughly Blue Rocket, were both good dogs. I cannot name them all so I will conclude with this tailpiece: the Smooth Collie is a great and noble breed, not all Smooths are born to be champions but all Smooths are born to be superb companions.


**JOAN E. HILL**
Mrs Hill is a north country woman born in Northumberland, and spent much of her childhood in Westmorland and Cumberland, has known the Smooth Collie all her life. A founder member, one-time chairman, and now vice-president of the Smooth Collie Club of Great Britain, Mrs Hill has owned and bred many champions in the breed both here in Britain and abroad. As president of the London Collie Club Mrs Hill is passed by the English Kennel Club to judge at championship level all three breeds of Collies. Apart from Collies Mrs Hill is a well-known breeder in Shetland Sheepdogs and lately has started a small kennel of Cavalier King Charles Spaniels. Many of the Smooth Collies mentioned in this book were known by Mrs Hill, and the Hewburn and the Redevalley strains have been known by her for many years.

# 4 The Bearded Collie
BY JOYCE COLLIS

The history of the Bearded Collie is hidden in the windswept hills and mountains of Scotland, Wales and Northern England. Odd scraps of information can be found by searching through old books, but the farmers, shepherds and drovers of days gone by were not educated men, and although sometimes their lives, and certainly their livelihood depended on their dogs, they thought no more of them than the sheep or cattle they minded. They kept few records, if any, of their pedigrees, and only stories of particular interest were handed down from father to son, and these were more than likely enlarged by repetition. They had worked and bred animals all their lives and by selective breeding they would have bred from dogs built for speed and stamina. The shepherd wanted a dog that could stand for hours guarding, and one that would travel miles guiding his flocks and not succumb to the driving wind and melting snow. He had to have a thick skin, warm undercoat and harsh topcoat to keep out the elements. He spent his lonely life in the Highlands working from early morning to late at night, tending his charges, and it did not matter to him if his coat was matted so long as he could work. The appearance of the dogs was of no importance to the shepherd as long as they had the intelligence to understand and obey without hesitation. They cared little if they were described as shaggy-haired, large-headed, large-eyed, big-nostrilled sheep-dogs, unkempt-looking, with coats like untidy doormats.

The spread of dog shows had gradually engulfed breed after breed, but had not reached the far northern counties. Shepherds and their working sheep-dogs did not as yet know or care about this pastime.

In the early twentieth century a Mr J. Dalgliesh, owner of a Bearded Collie named Ellwyn Garrie, seems to have been one of the first few to show and work his dogs. Ellwyn Garrie was a very dark slate dog, his coat was short and harsh, certainly not the texture and length of the present-day show specimen. He was large and heavy limbed, and as extra points were given for his working capabilities this would no doubt count for more than his general appearance. Lord Arthur Cecil's Ben was being shown also about this time, and although his colour was not described he seems more like the present-day Beardie, either fawn or light brown. From the photograph he looks a strong active animal.

When the Bearded Collie was beginning to be shown in beauty classes at shows it soon became important to formulate a standard. The first Bearded Collie Club was formed in 1912 and a standard was published by its members. Very little is known about this club, as before it became firmly established the First World War was declared and it did not survive.

In 1948 Mrs Willison (Bothkennar) registered the first Beardie with the Kennel Club, Jeannie of Bothkennar, well known to every dog owner as it is her head that is used as the trade mark for Vetzyme products. Mrs Willison became enamoured with the breed and she spent time, money and effort to set up the famous kennel of Bothkennar Bearded Collies. Her book, 'The Bearded Collie', gives all the details and the history of the Bothkennar dogs until 1963 so I shall only touch lightly on this period. Mr Sidney Green Swalehall had an unregistered Beardie which died in 1954; he searched everywhere for a replacement and finally saw an advertisement in the *Exchange and Mart* which read: 'Bearded bitch would exchange for gent's suit or seven pounds'. He sent the money immediately and camped out for three days on a platform at King's Cross; Swalehall Fly eventually arrived. She was passed for registration by Mrs Willison. There were several other Bearded Collie owners at that time but Mr Green is still a regular visitor to the Beardie rings and has just acquired another bitch.

In 1955 there were only eighteen registrations; this gradually increased until there was a sudden demand for Beardies, and in 1964 the registrations had spiralled to one hundred and twenty-one. Now in 1973 we are likely to see registrations of over four hundred. We now have a very active club, with more than four hundred members. In the past Beardies have been treated as quite a minor breed, having to accept judges who have not had the slightest idea of the breed standard, classing the dogs as 'sort of Old English Sheepdogs'. To the novice they might faintly resemble that breed, but to anyone who knows them they certainly do not. Firstly the coat is so completely different; the Beardie should have a straight or slightly wavy harsh topcoat with a good thick undercoat. The dog needs good bone but should not be too heavy; the back must be of fair length, but balanced, with an arched neck fitting on to well placed shoulders. The skull should be flat with ears set fairly high, and a strong long foreface with a moderate stop. Some of the dogs today do not have any stop at all, but camouflaged by the arched eyebrows this is not readily noticeable. The typical Beardie characteristics which attract so many are the alert, lively and self-confident temperament, the expression which can only be described as 'far seeing' and sometimes enquiring, a friendly lovable character (which admittedly can be boisterous if not checked at an early age). But channel its exuberance into obedience training, or ring craft training and you have a perfect house pet, wonderful companion and guard dog.

    I was first attracted to the Collie breed while watching two working sheep-dogs moving a flock of sheep along a narrow pathway in the very hilly country of Ayrshire during the war. They were working alone; there was no sign of a shepherd anywhere. I watched, fascinated. Years later while roaming around the show rings at Richmond

Championship Show I happened to pass the Bearded Collie rings. They looked out of place in those surroundings, and some were actively complaining by refusing to move properly; one of them raced across the ring as if he were working sheep. Another refused to be handled by the judge and continued to back away as he advanced. I admired their individuality and their distinct wildness. After months of enquiry I was able to buy my first Bearded Collie, a brown and white bitch called Gayfield Moonlight, from Mr and Mrs Banks of the Gayfield Kennels in Bury St Edmunds. Mrs Banks was an active breeder and exhibitor and has bred good quality Beardies since 1958; she has given me much advice and information about the breed. There were not many kennels in 1962 and very few one-pet owners who bred more than a single litter during the year. I searched the show catalogues and other than the Bothkennar, Willowmead (Miss Moorhouse), Cannamoor (Mrs Wheeler), Filabey (Mrs Anderson) and Wishanger (Miss Mary Partridge) there were no others to enquire about puppies. Early in 1964 I heard about a litter bred by Miss Morris of Binfield, her bitch Martha Scrope of Swalehall had produced one brown dog and five black and white bitches to Ch. Bosky Glen of Bothkennar.
I was able to take my pick of litter, and a very lucky choice it was because the puppy started winning at six months and when she was three became my champion Ella. Miss Jenifer Cooke bought another from this litter, a bitch called Scapa, and she became the first Bearded Collie obedience champion. By this time I really was captivated by this wonderful breed, and started another search for a dog, I wanted a sweet-tempered, dark slate, well built working type, and Jayemji Derhue answered all those requirements. I bought him from Mrs Janet Martineau of Tewkesbury (Jayemji Doona and Wishanger Wild Hyacinth).
Beardies were not as yet well known to the general public; in the show ring they were recognised more readily, but mostly when noticed were described as just a shaggy type of Old English Sheepdog. Then Players started an advertising campaign similar to the Dulux paint Old English Sheepdog, and Hushpuppy shoes featuring the

Basset Hound. Derhue was chosen from over one hundred dogs to look adoringly and trustingly up into the face of a young male model portraying the caption TRUST GOLD LEAF CIGARETTES TO TASTE GOOD. Other breeds had been used previously but they were well-known breeds such as the Golden Retriever, Irish Setter, Cocker Spaniel and Labrador. From ten-foot-high hoardings all over London and most of the major towns in Britain, Derhue's attractive handsome head with such expressive eyes brought the Bearded Collie to the notice of the masses. I was inundated with telephone calls and letters, asking for puppies from him, and received many requests to buy him at fabulous sums. Enquiries poured in to the Kennel Club, Players and my agents, asking what breed of dog he was, and where another could be bought like him. Since then more and more Beardies have been used for all manner of advertisements in the papers and on TV, they respond so readily to training and are keen to please, in general they just love people. Mrs Toni Teasedale's dog Osmart Black Bittern, and her two bitches Westernisles Sunset and Tonsarne Tatler are the photogenic Beardies used extensively on birthday cards and Christmas cards, biscuit tins and chocolate boxes. Sunset has also appeared in several TV commercials – Batchelor's soup and Lassie meaty chunks are two of her best known. If Mrs Teasedale is otherwise occupied when the bitch is required it presents no problems as Sunset will quite readily and happily work for any stranger. Vetzyme used the photograph of my Beagold Buzz and Jayemji Derhue to advertise their

Sally Anne Thompson

Vetzyme foam shampoo product. This particular foam shampoo is a boon to any owner of long-coated dogs but more of that later.

A Bearded Collie was used in a play on TV a few years back, quite an important part but one which caused quite a stir in the breed. This bitch had been left behind, while its owners went on holiday in the care of the next door neighbours, and as usually happens in such cases she was not properly cared for, and went roaming. Finally terrified by her experiences she is lost and attacks and kills an old tramp who is sleeping in a back alley recovering from the effects of drink. Then further to add to this incredulous story she attacks a child, stealing her lollipop. No one knowing the Beardie character would ever imagine any circumstances arising where a Beardie would attack to kill. This was definitely a blatant case of miscasting but no apologies were forthcoming. I don't think it did any harm to the good name of the Beardie although the breed name was mentioned. All that arises out of this remarkable story is that to portray a part so much out of character the bitch should have received a Doggy Oscar for her performance. History has repeated itself, and I could go on for hours recalling highly amusing and brilliantly clever stories where Beardies have been involved, leaving out the records made by some of our top show-quality dogs.

*Showing your Bearded Collie*
There are so many advantages gained if you join the Bearded Collie Club, the annual bounce-in is especially organised for the novice, although the non-beginners derive a great amount of pleasure from this get-together. Here you can meet other newcomers to the breed, and collect so much information about your dog. When he is six months old you can start entering him for shows, usually it is best to start at a local members limited show, although here you would only be offered Any Variety Pastoral, Any Variety Collie or Any Variety Working classes. These are fun to enter and surprisingly harder to win a card than in the open shows where Bearded Collies

are classified. If you feel confident and brave and want to jump in at the deep end, there are championship shows with challenge certificates offered for Beardies held in most of the big cities during the year. A win at a championship show can qualify for your entry to Cruft's. Watch the top breeders handle their dogs, whichever method of showing you prefer, practise at home and train your dog to respond to one or two commands, especially 'Stand'. The standard states that he should be alert, lively and self-confident, so encourage a little animation while the judge is looking in case he has read the standard. Asked to mention some of the 'all-time greats' in Bearded Collies that I have seen exhibited in my ten years with the breed, I would start my list with that handsome brown dog owned by Miss Mary Partridge, Ch. Wishanger Cairnbahn. Admittedly he reigned supreme when there were not so many dogs being shown, in fact, numbers were only on an average, five or six a class, but what a magnificent character! He has also sired so many litters to so many differently bred bitches, and still come up with top quality puppies. Even when he has been mated to close relations (in-breeding) no particularly noticeable faults have come to light in the offspring. His characteristic entry into the open class at Cruft's 1973, at ten and a half years of age was a joy to behold, he greeted everyone and exuded happiness at his familiar surroundings. Another, quieter, but proud character was that outstanding dog Ch. Bracken Boy of Bothkennar, retired now, owned by Miss Shirley Holmes. When he came into the ring it was a foregone conclusion that here was the challenge certificate winner. In all he won fifteen. In his younger days he did not just move, he flowed over the ground, his outline was perfect, his mien superb. Miss Suzanne Moorhouse's Will O'Wisp of Willowmead was another stud and show dog that made an impact on the breed, he won two challenge certificates and three reserve and was best in show at the Midland Collie Club in 1958. Then for personal reasons Miss Moorhouse was out of the show rings for a few years, but if his show career had remained uninterrupted he would have easily gained his title. The well-known blue,

Ch. Osmart Bonnie Blue Braid, owned by Miss Catherine Osborne, needs no further introduction, a handsome, masculine-looking dog who has won eleven challenge certificates and thirteen best of breeds. He is another that is dominant, and it is so easy to pick out his progeny, as so many seem to have his outstanding head. My first view of Mrs Barbara Iremonger's Ch. Sunbrees Magic Moments of Willowmead was at one of the bounce-ins, he was the type that gave the name to that particular get-together, he was full of fun and life, and seemed to bubble over. Later on in his show career after he had settled down, there was no mistaking his excellent points, and gorgeous coat. It was not surprising that he was soon made up to a champion. Miss Shirley Holmes is now showing her home-bred, top quality blue Ch. Edenborough Blue Bracken, he topped off his wins throughout the year by going best of breeds at Cruft's 1973.

My bitch list would without doubt have two at the top, Mrs Jackie Tidmarsh's glamorous brown Ch. Edelweiss of Tambora, she has won six challenge certificates and three reserve. She was best in show at the Bearded Collie Club in 1969 and winner of the Tambora Points Trophy for that same year. Also Mrs Diane Hale's Ch. Broadholme

Adorable, a beautiful black and white bitch has produced some top quality puppies. As always happens with bitches they make a brief appearance, especially the outstanding ones, win their three challenge certificates to make them champions, then retire for their maternal duties. There have been so many that I can only name a few. Miss Suzanne Moorhouse's Ch. Broadholme Cindy Sue of Willowmead who was top bitch of 1968. Miss Patricia Gilpin's Ch. Wishanger Waterfall top bitch of 1970. All these have left the ring to have puppies, and surprisingly few return. That is why it is much easier to make up a bitch champion than a dog. The top quality dogs are stayers, and remain in showing condition sometimes into their sixth year, perhaps slowing down a little but usually in remarkably top quality fitness passing on into the veteran classes.

*Preparing for Show*
It is very seldom that a judge remarks about a badly groomed Bearded Collie these days. Most are extremely well presented, and look as if hours of brushing and grooming have gone into their shiny coats, with the white which can be described as 'whiter than white'. There are so many show preparations to assist, all that is needed is time, and dry weather to keep a Beardie in tip-top show condition. I cannot count the number of times that I have set off for a show with my dogs sparkling with cleanliness only to arrive at the show ground to find a sea of mud surrounding the car park and every access road into the show. This is when the Vetzyme foam shampoo comes in useful, rubbed in, towelled off, then rubbed in again and talcum powder rubbed in the damp foot, the coat soon looks clean again. All this is, of course, for the day of the show, but 'preparing for showing' starts when a puppy is about eight weeks old. I get the puppy used to all my grooming paraphernalia, brushes, combs, etc., toothbrush and scraper, nail cutters, and especially inspection of ears. I prefer to groom on a table so I stand the puppy on the table and handle him firmly saying gently 'Stand'. They soon get used to the brush and comb, in fact, my juniors

try to push in as soon as the other is finished and I end up
with about three on the table before their turn. Beardies
do always need regular grooming, or the tangles soon
appear, behind the ears, under the front legs, and under the
tail. If this is not done regularly, there is a massive attack
needed on the coat the week before the show, and it shows!
Looking around the rings you can soon pick out the dogs
that have their coats regularly attended to, and the broken
coats of those that have had to have great big matts
taken out. Also some Beardies take to showing like a duck
to water, they enjoy the journey to the show, doesn't
matter how far they have come, they enjoy the bustle and
noise of the big cities, and jump on to their benches with
such enthusiasm, then greet every passer-by like a long-lost
friend. Then there are the others that change completely
in character at the very mention of 'Show', won't
co-operate in any way, won't get on to their bench,
certainly will not walk properly in the ring and then take
an instant dislike to the judge. This is usually the best dog
you have in your kennels, you could shake it, but it won't
do any good. I have one like that, he slinks around the
show ring as if he has a regular daily whipping, he hates
to be benched. At home he is the sweetest tempered, most
lovable character, also sticks up for his rights with the
other dogs, never needs chastisement, and obediently
comes when he is called. He loves to jump up on
everything above ground, and sits quite happily
precariously perched on a high wall, so it is not heights
that he dislikes. He just does not like shows.

*Picking your Beardie Puppy*
When buying your Beardie puppy choose one that has a
shiny, healthy-looking coat, bright clean eyes, no discharge
from its nostrils, and a clean rear end. If it is to be a show
dog assess its good points and whether at that age (eight
weeks) you think it has a good temperament, a certain
amount of character and finally the colour you want. I
have had customers book a puppy which 'must have a
white collar, white blaze and perfectly marked, it must
also be silver grey, not too much coat, but, of course, not

too little', and another will just want a good Beardie.
If I am picking a born black puppy, I like to see a dark eye, if, of course, both parents are silver grey I allow the eye to be slightly lighter as the standard says that 'Eyes – To tone with coat in colour'. The pigmentation on the other hand must be black, especially around the eye rims and nose. A flat, well-shaped skull with ears not set too high, a slight stop, with well-placed eyes and fullness in the cheeks. The muzzle must at this age be strong and rounded, a kindly sweet expression which when seen is never forgotten. I like my puppy to be well shaped in body, nice length of back and especially a balanced length of neck. Even at this age the slight arch is noticeable. Of course, a tail that curls over the back all the time is not likely to be in the proper position later on, so I would not pick one with that particular fault unless it was outstanding in all other aspects, that would mean I would have to train it to carry its tail down, it can be done but I would rather choose another if that were possible. Good bone is also essential, but not too heavy or coarse, as that puppy could well turn out to be the Old English type. A well-rounded, plump, but not too fat, puppy has a better chance of facing up to its new owner, its strange surroundings and settling in with no problems than a poor looking thin little creature which might still be very wormy. Ask for a menu as a change of diet could well retard a healthy puppy's growth. The great upheaval of leaving its mother and familiar surroundings is enough for it to cope with without being given a completely new diet. Continue the regular training and grooming, make it a pleasant time for the puppy, he will then only have happy memories of your time spent together, it should never be a fight from start to finish with both feeling hot and bothered and out of temper.

*Breeding from your bitch*
It is an absolute fallacy that a bitch must have a litter to keep her healthy. If I receive an enquiry for the use of my stud dogs, and the person seems the slightest bit doubtful that she really can cope with a litter, but thinks it would

be good for the bitch, I always try to discuss the matter, putting forward the difficulties, the time and trouble, and enlarging on the fact that it might be impossible to sell the puppies from a novice breeder. If it is another puppy they want I suggest they buy one in, rather than produce a lot more that might not be placed in suitable homes.

If, however, they insist that it is a litter of their own that they want I then try to help all I can. The ideal time to breed from a Bearded Collie bitch is her third season, or when she is about 18 months to two years old. Study her pedigree, and if the bitch was bought from a well-known breeder, it is best to write there for advice as to the best mate for your particular bitch. Most breeders will be only too pleased to advise. When you have decided on the choice of stud dog contact the owner in good time. A keen stud dog and a willing bitch present no problems for the breeder, on the other hand there may be no end of trouble encouraging the dog to serve the bitch, or the bitch to accept the dog, so it is a wise policy to have a person present who has lots of experience in these matters. Beardie dogs are usually dead keen to mate a bitch, at any time, and very few bitches refuse the advances of a vigorous stud dog.

Prepare the whelping quarters well before the puppies are due, I find that lots of newspaper in a whelping box forty-four inches by thirty-four inches, and an infra-red lamp is all that is needed, the rest of the warmth is provided by the mother, and usually Beardies make marvellous mothers, and are easy whelpers. Although I always stay up, or if during the day stay with my bitch during the whole time. There might come the time when help is needed, and if so I want to be there. I also usually decide which puppy I am going to keep at birth, it is so much easier to pick from your own bred pups, especially if you have planned the mating by either line or in-breeding. You then know what to expect and can decide what to discard and what to put high on your priorities.

I handle my pups as often as possible, talk to them, and check over them from the day they are born. When their eyes open at about ten days they see as much of me nearly as often as their own mother. I start to wean at about two to three weeks – it all depends if there is more than six in the litter. I hold a ball of doubled minced meat in my fingers and with the puppy on my lap encourage it to suck at the meat, some need no encouragement, but others are reluctant to accept this new taste, and search around for the familiar smell of their mother's milk. I persevere and before a couple of days pass they are attacking frantically a little dish of meat now fed twice a day. I prefer to feed the pups in individual bowls as no two pups eat at the same speed. I do not like to see tiny pups paddling around in one large dish and there is no way to check that each pup is getting the right amount of food. A greedy one could be tightly packed and near to bursting, and another shy feeder reluctant to tackle the gooey mass. By this time most Beardie mothers have found other interests, and need a lot of encouragement to go in with the pups during the day, although happily stay with them during the night.

*Conclusion*
Those that choose a Beardie for their companion need not think that they are going to continue leading a sedentary

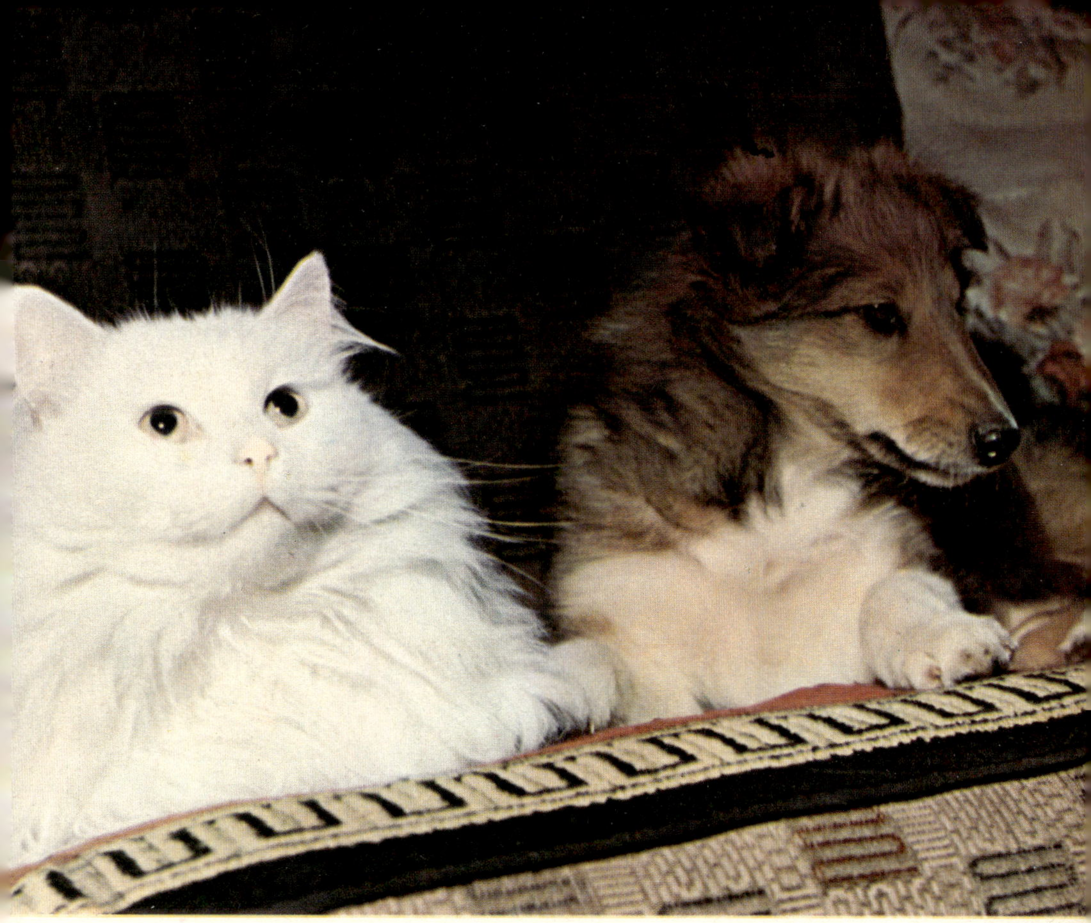

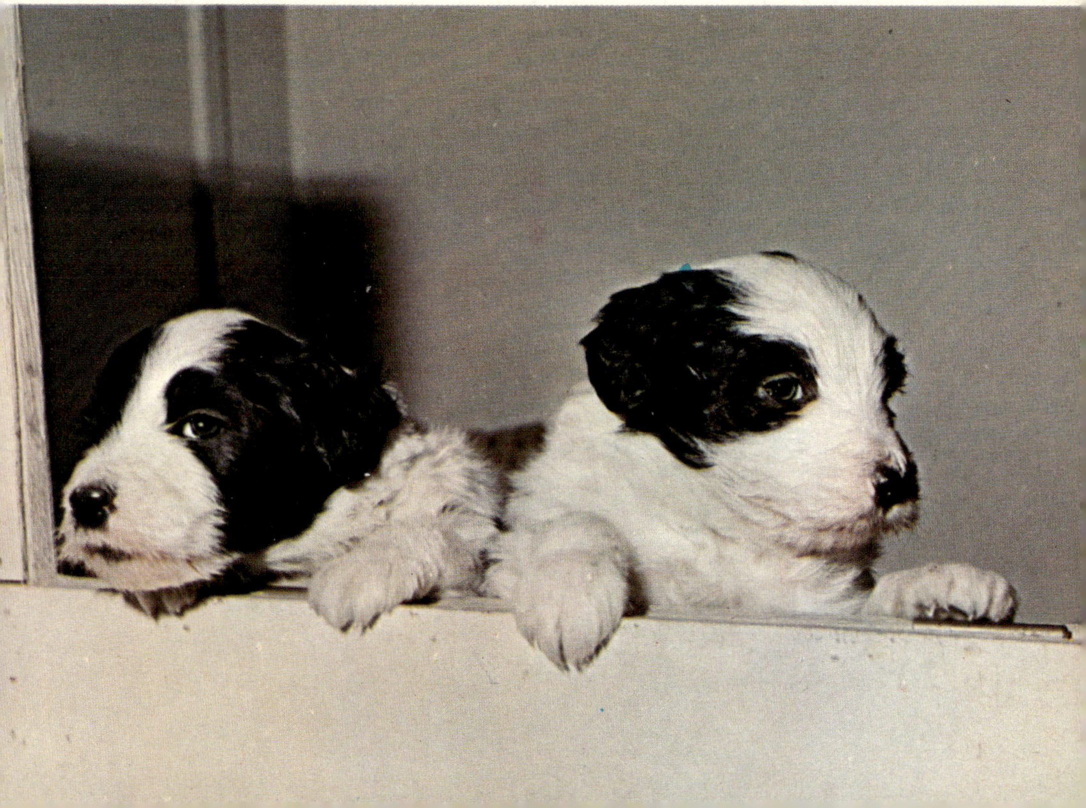

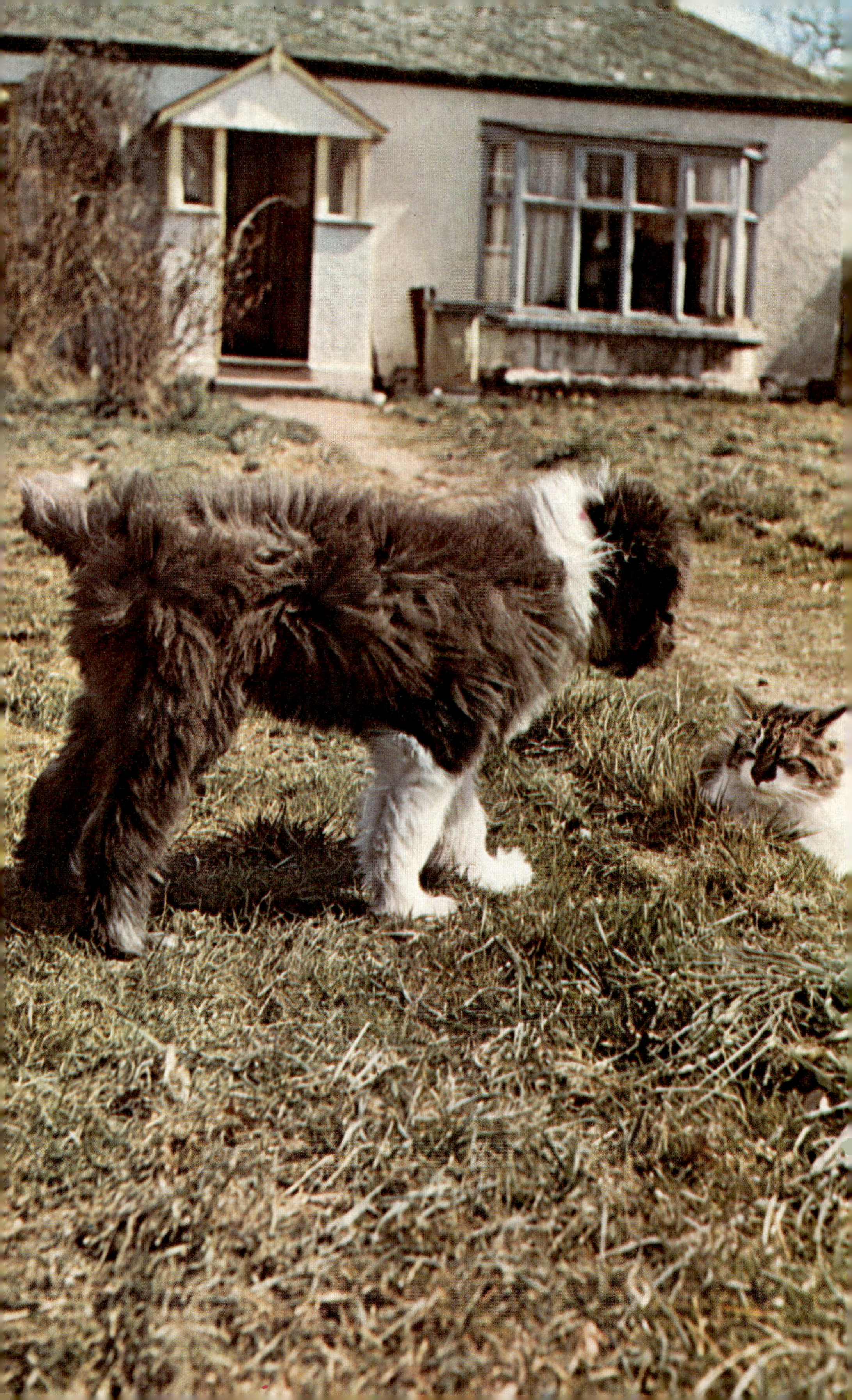

life in the future. All that will be altered. Rain, hail,
wind or snow will not provide an excuse to stay by the fire.
It is not done by fair means, but definitely foul. Settle
yourself by a roaring blaze, a good dog book and tit-bits to
chew, or make plans to watch a good TV show and see
what happens. Not a tap on your leg, no pleading eyes
boring into your back, no wagging tail demanding your
attention so that you can viciously whisper 'Get down, and
go away'. No, the gentle tap, the pleading eyes, the
expectant 'walk-look' is directed at the master of the house.
Never in a million years do they expect him to get out of
his comfortable chair, and brave the elements, no, it is
done for a reason. 'Don't you think these dogs want their
walk dear?' Never imagine that the enjoyment of their
walk is lessened by the freezing conditions, not on your
life, they are as entranced by the wintery spect as they are
by everything else that is difficult to cope with by a normal
human being. They are just Beardies!

**JOYCE COLLIS**
A life-long interest in dogs, Mrs Collis was five when her family's
first bitch had puppies. Dolls were thrown away, the pram filled
with puppies and she was hooked. Went to her first dog show in
1950 and had to be fetched away late in the evening, having
been there all day just watching and lapping up the atmosphere.
Read everything possible and visited every dog event in the
district before finally taking the plunge as an exhibitor. First
started with a Cocker Spaniel and then went on to breed Beagles
and Golden Retrievers for several years before finally settling
for the Bearded Collie. Until three years ago always lived in
the town, but is now settled in the country with her husband and
family. Dreams have finally come true in the shape of a country
cottage, two kennel blocks, a whelping and mating room, and
tries to keep the number of Beardies to about ten. A founder
member of the North Herts Dog Training Club and secretary for
a number of years. On the committee of the Hitchin Canine
Society, and held the post of secretary for seven years. In 1965
joined the committee of the Bearded Collie Club of England. A
most successful breeder of Beardies, Mrs Collis is also a
championship show judge of the breed.

# 5 Training

BY JOHN HOLMES

The first essential in training is not patience or love of animals as so many people think. And it is not a knowledge of how to make a dog sit, lie down, or take up any other position, as some books would have us believe. The first essential is what I call dog sense – a knowledge of canine mentality – giving one the ability to understand what makes a dog tick.

The reason why the dog is so much easier to train than the cat (which has been domesticated for just as long) is not because it is more intelligent. It is because the dog is a pack animal while the cat prefers a more or less solitary existence. In a pack of dogs there is a very highly developed social order with a leader and followers in a very definite order – top dogs and underdogs, so to speak. One also finds top cats and undercats but there is a vast difference. Whereas the underdogs actually obey and follow their leaders, an undercat simply keeps out of the way of a top cat. The dog's natural instinct is, therefore, to obey a leader, while a cat only wants to please itself, which means that a dog can be made to do certain things we want even when he does not like doing them, while a cat can only be persuaded to do the things it likes doing.

One of the most remarkable features of the domestic dog is the extent to which it still retains the mental characteristics of its wild ancestry. Man has created a larger variety of canine types than in any other domestic species. It is hard to believe that the Pekingese and the Great Dane, the Chihuahua and the Irish Wolfhound all have the same common ancestry. By looking at them one could be excused for saying 'It's impossible!'. But by studying their mental make-up one becomes more and more aware of the similarity in all breeds. Of course different breeds, produced for different jobs, have certain differences in mentality but they are not nearly as great as is generally believed. It is certainly much less than the different opinions of their breeders. Ask a dedicated breeder of *any* breed and he or she will tell you that it is definitely different from *all* other breeds and of course better in every way. And these people honestly believe what they say for the simple reason that they have never owned any other breed and are so wrapped up in their own that they never even see the breed being judged in the next ring at a dog show. I mention this because I believe that much confusion in training is caused by the idea that each breed has a completely different mentality.

In my time I have trained many dogs for many purposes – film dogs, gun dogs, sheepdogs, guard dogs, working terriers, etc., and I have found that the basic principles of training apply to all dogs of all breeds and indeed to all animals.

The first principle is that by nature the dog wants a leader that it can respect and obey. And he is quite willing, indeed grateful, to be led by a human pack leader. This does not mean that dogs are almost human and it is a dreadful insult to the canine species to suggest that they are. It simply means that we are all animals and many of us are capable of taking on the rôle of pack leader, providing that we are more intelligent and stronger willed than the animal we want to obey us. That many are not is evidenced by the number of disobedient, trouble-making dogs to be seen everywhere.

Here we have a two-way problem. The majority of dogs are what is known as submissive and want to follow a leader but a few are born to be leaders and are known as dominant dogs. Exactly the same happens in the human race and, although we do not usually talk about dominant and submissive people, many readers will know what I mean. The problem usually arises from the fact that a submissive person can rarely train a dominant dog. It is for this reason that a dog will often obey one member of the family and not another. Normally a dog obeys the father first, the mother second and treats young children as equals. But sometimes the dog will obey the mother and take no notice of what the father says. I have invariably found in such cases that the husband obeys the wife too! A dominant person rarely gets the same pleasure from a submissive dog as from a fairly dominant one. Although easy to train to a high standard I get little pleasure from training submissive dogs. All the dogs which stand out in my memory as 'greats' have been dominant, many of them bloody-minded awkward brutes which had been discarded by their previous owners.

This is not a chapter on how to choose a dog but, if you have not already bought one, you should pay particular attention to this point. A person who cannot train one dog may get another *of the same breed* and train it to perfection. Likewise the dog which that person failed to train may go to someone else who will train it quite easily.

The next principle is that dogs do not reason as we do. Here there is considerable difference of opinion. On the one hand there are scientists who say that man is the only animal which reasons. On the other there are people who claim that their dog not only understands every word they say to it but actually talks to them as well, and they carry on regular conversations. Most scientists study dogs under clinical conditions which are quite unnatural. Nothing could be more unnatural than the conditions under which the average domestic dog lives but these are still very different from laboratory conditions, and many pet owners are so preoccupied with turning their dearly beloved into a four-legged human being that they really do believe it does many of the stupid things people do and they never allow it to do any of the clever things which dogs can do.

In my opinion dogs do sometimes reason to a considerable extent. But we cannot really say to what extent and, as the dog cannot tell us, it is unlikely that we shall ever know. What trainers have learned from experience is that to attempt to train an animal is doomed to failure if it is assumed that it can reason. All training must, therefore, be based on the assumption that *dogs do not reason.*

Dogs learn by association of ideas. They associate certain sounds or sights with pleasure or displeasure. They tend to do the things naturally which result in pleasure and refrain from those which create displeasure. I believe that a dog associates sounds and sights in exactly the same way as we do. All of us can think of a tune, the sound of waves breaking on the seashore, gunfire, a police car siren or one of many other sounds which bring back vivid memories –

pleasant or unpleasant – every time we hear them. Likewise with things we have seen and the same sight and sound may well bring back either pleasant or unpleasant memories, like the sight of a telegram messenger who may bring either good or bad news. The most important thing to remember is that the more pleasant or unpleasant the experience the stronger the association of ideas. To most of us a telegram does not do very much but those who have received tragic news by telegram become apprehensive, even terrified, of opening another one. In the same way, those who have received glad tidings by telegram will not be apprehensive of receiving one in the future, knowing quite well that it may not bring good news.

The strongest association is built up by fear. If a child gets bitten by a dog it will be excused for having a lifetime fear of dogs. But if a puppy gets kicked by a child people will wonder why it develops a lifelong fear of children and the breeder will be accused of selling a dog with a bad temperament.

First associations are usually much stronger than subsequent ones. If a child has a very unpleasant experience on the first day at school he or she may take a long time to get over it. If this had not occurred until several weeks at school had passed, it might have had little or no effect. People who show dogs know that if a puppy gets a bad fright at its first show it may dislike shows for life. The same experience a year later might have no effect at all.

Another point worth remembering is that dogs, like us, are much more easily upset and with much more lasting effect when they are off colour. An experience which would have little or no effect under normal circumstances can have disastrous results if it happens when a puppy is teething or has a virus infections, or when a bitch is in season, especially for the first time, and in many cases the animal shows no real symptoms of illness.

For training purposes we try to create the association of ideas which we want in the dog and we do it by correction and reward. This means that we try to make it unpleasant for the dog to do the things we don't want him to do and pleasant for him to do the things we do want. The best example of how we should do this is to be seen by studying a bitch with puppies. First of all she supplies them with food from her own mammary glands and later partly digested food which she regurgitates for them. She also licks and caresses them and makes friendly soft noises which fall somewhere between grunting and whining. The puppies, therefore, associate her with food and caressing and every time they see, hear or smell her they rush joyously to her, just as everyone hopes their new puppy will rush to them; if they feed it, fondle and pet it and make friendly noises to it the chances are that this will happen.

    Most people in fact do this, overlooking the fact that the bitch's training does not end there. As the puppies become bigger the bitch, without losing interest in them, does not want to be mauled about by them all the time. Many dog owners put up with that but bitches usually have more sense! So, when the puppies become a bit overbearing the bitch growls at them. Many pups react instinctively to a growl and will stop what they are doing, be it chewing the mother's ear or tail or trying to suckle when there is no milk at the bar, but some bold, dominant pups pay little or no attention. The bitch then repeats her threat and, if there is no response, she will snap at the puppy, often hurting it quite badly by human standards. But she does not hurt it often. Next time the puppy hears an angry growl it associates it with a snap and quickly responds. If it does not, it gets another and another until it *does* respond. When a bitch snaps at a puppy it usually gets a fright and runs away a little distance. But it soon crawls back to be licked and caressed and will soon be happy again.

From this I hope you will realise that far from being unnatural, as some people would have us believe, training is the most natural thing in the world, and the bitch with her puppies (many other animals are similar) is an excellent example of simple and straightforward association of ideas. Once upon a time dogs and children were trained according to these simple principles. We have now become more highly educated and use big words like psychiatrist and psychoanalysis – we even have canine psychologists who have never kept a dog in their lives – and everywhere we find disobedient and unhappy dogs and children.

The dog has a simple straightforward mind. He is highly intelligent but less intelligent than we are. If you are less intelligent than your dog just forget about trying to train him! Most of his senses and instincts are far stronger than ours. He sees as well as we do but, because he is nearer the ground and cannot see what we see, many people say his sight is inferior. He hears many times better than we do but from the shouting at many training classes one could believe that all dogs were deaf. His memory is as good if not better than ours, yet people will marvel at their dog recognising them after a six-week holiday. It would be just as logical to be unable to recognise one's own family – and the dog – after that period. Bearing all the above facts in mind let us now try to apply them to the new puppy you have just bought.

To start with remember that he is only a baby suddenly removed from his mother and probably his brothers and sisters too. At this stage he does not want a leader as much as a comforter to replace his mother. Generally speaking women are much better than men at giving confidence to young animals and it is fortunate that in most households it is the woman who takes the new puppy under her wing. This is not just an idea of my own. The Guide Dogs for the Blind Association employs girls to look after the puppies and to do the initial training while men take over the more advanced training when the dog is old enough to need a leader.

You may have noticed when I was talking about creating associations of ideas I said that we *try* to create those we want and avoid those we do not want. But many wrong associations are built up by ignorance or accident. So far as the new puppy is concerned it is more important to avoid wrong associations than to attempt to create ones we want. Remember what I said about first associations and associations which are created when the animal's resilience is low. A young puppy is much more likely to forget an experience whether pleasant or unpleasant than an older one, but any animal is much more likely to get a bad fright in unfamiliar surroundings than in familiar ones.

Many dogs, I believe, have their temperaments completely ruined the first week they go to a new home as a result of the owner's misguided and often cruel attempts to house train them. A human baby is wrapped in nappies and even an older child is excused of wetting its bed if it is worried or upset, for example when he or she has to stay in a strange house. But a canine baby, which probably has never been in a house and which has been taken from its familiar environment by people it has never seen before, is expected to last all night without making a mistake. When it does it has its nose rubbed in it and probably smacked into the bargain. The owner than says 'I can't understand it. When I brought him home he was so friendly and rushed to greet me. Now he runs and hides every times he sees me'. What would you do if someone treated you like that?

Quite apart from the mental and physical suffering caused to the puppy this method has nothing to commend it. It is highly unlikely that the puppy will associate the punishment with the 'crime' which it could not avoid anyhow. There is, however, every likelihood that it will associate the punishment with the person who administers it and/or the place where it occurred. By persisting in this treatment it is possible to turn a normal bold puppy into a complete nervous wreck in less time than you could believe possible. I know dogs do survive this treatment with no apparent ill effects but they have exceptional temperaments in the first place.

The first object therefore should be to get the puppy to like you. And you can't make a dog like you any more than you can a person. All you can do is try to be a likeable person in the eyes of the dog by doing the things he likes. A young puppy likes being cuddled, fondled and petted, but not all the time. He wants to run about and play and chew things up. But you don't want him to chew the house to pieces so give him something to play with. Like all young animals he not only wants but needs to sleep. We all know how lack of sleep frays our nerves, making us irritable and bad tempered, but many puppies are kept continually awake because the owner wants to pet or play with them. Children are allowed, even encouraged to run around chasing a puppy often terrifying the life out of it. They give it no peace and one day they get bitten, which serves them right; but it is the puppy which is put down and the children are given another one to torment. If you can't train your children it is unlikely you will train a dog. So, save it a lot of suffering by not having it at all.

These are only a few of the many examples of how unpleasant associations can be created by ignorance and lack of consideration. There can still be accidents. Small puppies, especially friendly ones, are adept at getting under one's feet and it is no good saying that it was his own fault that he got trodden on. A puppy does not reason like that and to him you are just an enormous animal towering above him with a huge foot which causes severe pain when plonked on top of him. There are lots of other things which can happen to puppies like doors being slammed on them and furniture falling on top of them, all of which can have a disastrous and sometimes lasting effect.

The best way to avoid unpleasant experiences to the puppy and at the same time save yourself some unpleasant experiences is to provide a playpen. This can be on the lines of a child's play pen and need not be elaborate or expensive. All that is necessary is an enclosure large enough to give a fair amount of freedom and strong enough to prevent the escape of the puppy in question. As there is so much variation in puppies and the conditions applying to different households I shall not attempt to describe the construction of a play pen. The puppy's bed should be placed in the pen. There is a wide variety of beds on the market, such as baskets, ideal for a puppy to chew to pieces. To the puppy an old tea chest or other box on its side is just as good if not better, as it is more enclosed. A board nailed across the front will stop any floor draught and help to keep in an old piece of blanket or other material for bedding. Some newspaper should be spread on the floor of the pen.

 The advantage of a play pen should be obvious. While it not only prevents the creation of many undesirable associations of ideas, it also prevents the development of several bad habits. In very few households is there anyone with the time (even if they had the inclination) to keep a constant eye on a puppy. If he is in his pen he cannot mess on the best carpet, chew up the best slippers (they always choose the best ones), get trodden on or jammed in the door. Most important of all he won't get on your nerves or you on his.

If the puppy needs to relieve itself it will use the newspaper which can be picked up without any fuss and bother. Not that I advocate encouraging the puppy to use it play pen as a lavatory! The sooner a puppy is house trained the sooner it is likely to become a pleasant member of the household but there is rarely any need for drastic methods so often advocated. And no correction should be applied until the puppy is happy in its new surroundings and has complete confidence in its new owner. This may take an hour with an exceptionally bold puppy brought up in a house or perhaps two or three days with a less bold puppy reared in a kennel. An eight-week-old puppy should be completely confident in three days, if not there is something wrong either with the pup or the new home. Generally speaking the older a dog is the longer it will take to settle down and the more effect its previous upbringing will have. For instance, a pup reared from eight weeks in a home with children can at six months go to another home with children and settle down right away, but the same pup if reared in a home with a quiet elderly couple, or in kennels with a lot of other dogs, might never get over the shock of a house full of noisy children. We have found that one of the worst ages to change a puppy's environment is between four and five months old when it is teething.

To return to the question of house training few people realise that the average puppy wants to be clean in its own living quarters. All animals born in nests learn at quite an early age to go out of the nest to relieve themselves, thereby keeping their living quarters clean. The object should be to develop this instinct which can usually be done without any correction at all and certainly without the brutal treatment so often administered.

The first essential is an observant owner. Because of its instinct to be clean nearly every puppy will show symptoms of wanting to relieve itself. Unfortunately few owners recognise these symptoms and expect the puppy to ask to go out by whimpering or even barking. The most usual symptom is when the puppy simply starts looking around and probably sniffing the floor. When this happens take him out, wait until he has done what he has to do, praise him well and bring him back in. Don't just push him out and shut the door. He may well have decided that the door mat was the ideal place for his purpose and wait on the doorstep until the door opens, when he will come in and do what he intended doing exactly where he intended doing it. If you do catch a puppy actually in the act of squatting down pick him up firmly by the scruff say 'No' or 'Bad boy' in a corrective tone (the equivalent of his mother's growl) and take him out. To a young puppy this is *very* severe correction and should be done quietly without any shouting or flapping of folded newspapers so often recommended.

   The important thing is to catch the puppy in the act and this rule applies to all training. Correction after the event (even seconds after) is unlikely to do any good and more than likely to do a great deal of harm. Remember that we are trying to work on the dog's mind and not his body and he will associate correction with what is on his mind at the time. For instance if a dog is corrected when he is looking at a cat with the obvious intention of chasing it that should be very effective. If he is corrected as he is chasing the cat that should be effective too. But if he chases a cat up a tree and you correct him when he returns to you, you will have corrected him for coming back, not for chasing cats. In this way many dogs are taught by their owners *not* to come back when called – and they still chase cats!

In the same way many puppies become afraid of owners who leave them alone for hours then return and punish them for wetting on the floor – which the poor little blighter could not avoid anyway. 'Of course he knows,' they say. 'Just see how guilty he looks.' But he does not look guilty at all, he simply looks afraid and with very good reason. You can prove this for yourself by scolding any reasonably sensitive dog when it has done nothing wrong and it will immediately look 'guilty' through fear or apprehension.

If one has to leave a puppy for a long period, put him in his play pen and of course he can sleep in it at night. All one has to do then is pick up the soiled newspaper. As he gets older he should learn to wait until he is let out and should be able to do so. A puppy accustomed to newspaper will sometimes prefer to use it in preference to going out. If you take it up and keep an eye on him you should notice when he goes looking for it and take that as a signal to let him out.

Our own dogs are never house trained in the generally accepted sense but simply encouraged to develop their instinct to be clean. Some live in the house and some in kennels and it is rare indeed for an adult to make a mistake in either. They work in studios, live with us in a motor caravan and often stay in hotels and the only problem we ever have is when a director wants a dog to lift its leg in the studio! Having been encouraged to be clean very few of our dogs will do this indoors but will readily oblige outside on the studio lot.

Dog training cannot be divided into compartments and it

is useless deciding to spend a fortnight on one exercise and then a fortnight on another. All training must synchronise and a lot of it has to take place simultaneously. There are however, certain 'exercises' which must be learnt before going on to other exercises. These are the basic exercises and the important point about them is that once the teacher and the pupil understand them thoroughly they can go on to more advanced exercises at any time – even after a lapse of several years. Space being limited I intend to deal only with the basic exercises. By the time you have mastered them I hope you will be keen enough on training to buy a book and proceed to more advanced training.

My reason for starting with house training is not because it is more important than other exercise or because it should be taught first. Indeed it is the only exercise which is of no benefit to anyone except the owner – or his friends who visit his house – which is probably why the average owner is so much keener on house training than on teaching the dog not to bite the postman! And that is why I started with it – because it is the first thing most people want to know about. There is actually another reason for starting house training soon after a puppy goes to a new home. A puppy with a strong instinct to be clean will soon choose a secluded spot as a 'loo' and will always go there. If that happens to be at the bottom of the garden it's fine. But if it happens to be behind the piano or the couch in the best room that's not so funny. And if an idea like that (based on an instinct) is allowed to develop it can be very difficult to change. All training must endeavour to create good habits and prevent bad ones.

One good habit which the puppy should learn right from the start is to come when called. In spite of everything you believe or have been told about dogs that 'understand every word said to him' dogs do not in fact, understand any words at all. They simply recognise sounds (far more accurately than we do) and they associate these sounds with certain actions. If your dog gets excited when you mention 'Walk' it is simply because he associates that sound (not a word to him) with going for a walk. Instead of recognising that simple fact dog owners resort to spelling the word. Very soon the dog associates the sounds W-A-L-K with going for a walk and his owners think he has learnt to spell!

At this stage we are mainly concerned with encouraging the puppy to come to us in response to a particular sound. The sound is usually the dog's name and where there are a lot of dogs, such as we keep, it is important that each and every one responds to its own name and to no other. But we do not go around repeating a dog's name over and over again for no reason at all. We use the dog's name when we want him to come to us – and if we don't want him we don't call him. The average owner, however, appears unable to desist from repeating the puppy's name every time he sees it. Not only that – the whole family, friends and neighbours will want to have cosy chats with any new puppy repeating its name over and over again in the process. Any new puppy we get will come to us in response to its name within a day or two but the average puppy hears its name so much that it completely ignores the sound just as it does the sound of the radio or television.

Constantly repeated sounds without association become ignored. For that reason it is often advisable to teach a dog to come to you in response to a different sound altogether like 'here' or 'come'. The word matters not and it is just as easy to teach a dog to come by saying 'go' as by saying 'come'. What does matter is that you always use the same command and use it in the right tone of voice. As I said earlier, a puppy instinctively cowers or even runs away at the sound of its mother's growl and will rush to greet her when she makes her soft welcoming noise, which is almost inaudible to human ears. The ability to change the tone of voice is vital in training and is one of the gifts which divides successful trainers into successful and unsuccessful. Don't confuse tone with volume. It is never necessary to shout at a puppy in the confines of its own house.

Now we come to the big question. How do you teach this charming puppy to rush to you in joyous bounds every time you call it? To start with you want to persuade rather than try to make it come. Later you may have to make him (he may have lost some of his charm by then!) but try persuasion first.

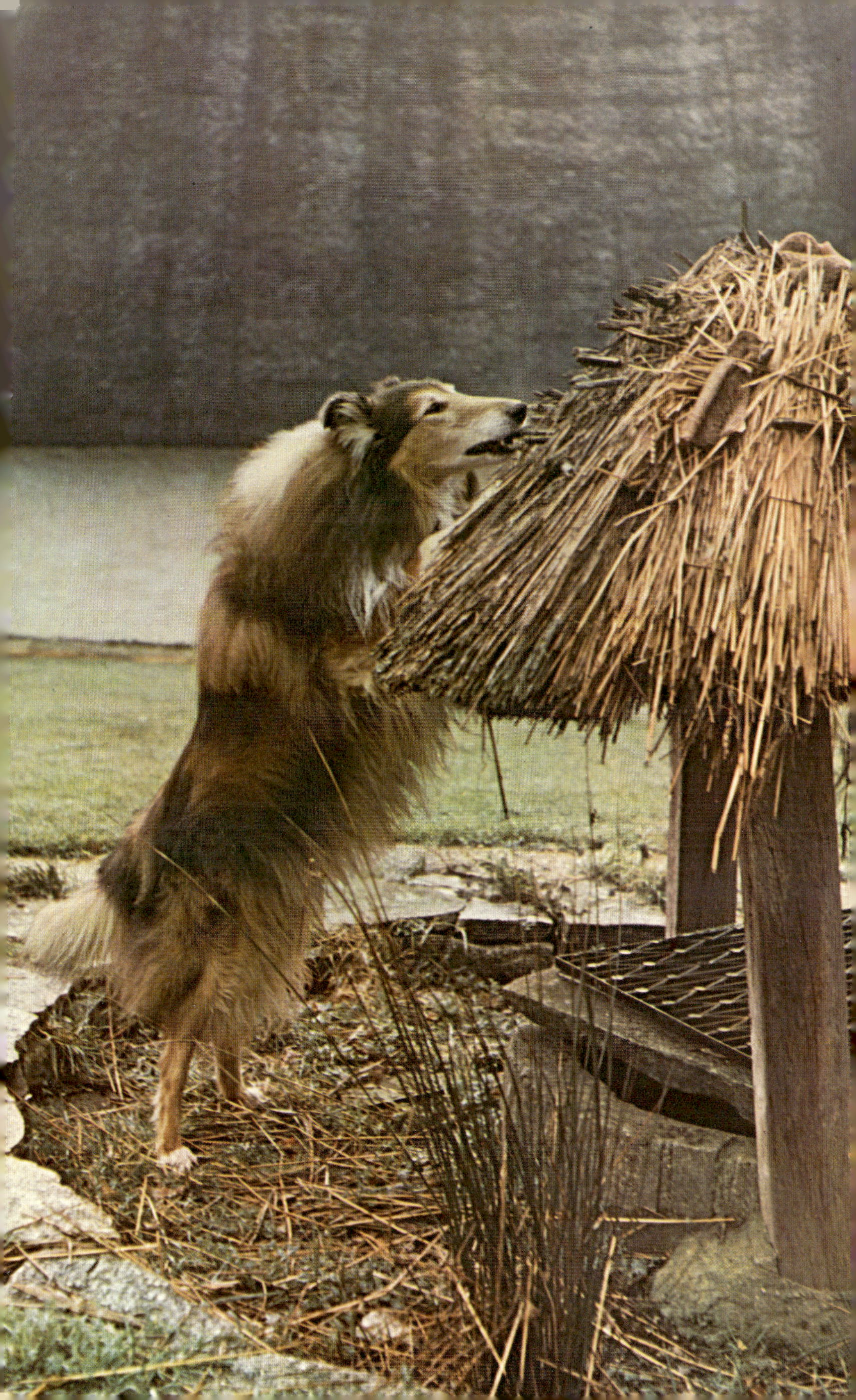

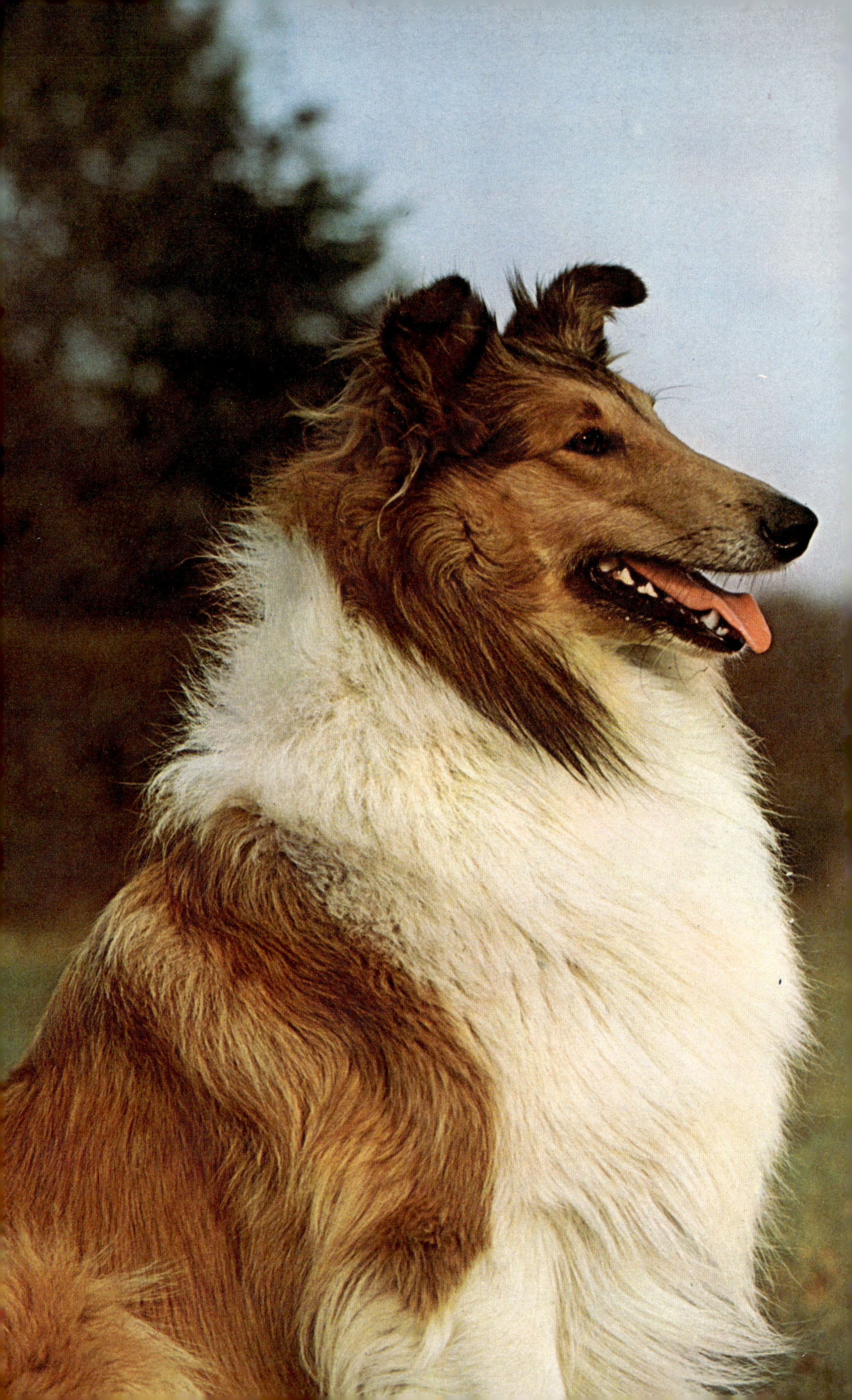

Obviously you should start by calling the puppy in a nice friendly persuasive tone of voice, never in a harsh correcting tone. If you stand straight up he is likely to stand back staring at the great thing towering above him but if you squat down he should come up to you even if you do not ask him.

A timid puppy will move away every time you move towards him but is almost certain to come nearer if you move away from him.

An outstretched hand with moving fingers will attract nearly any puppy, and many adult dogs, while the same hand with fist clenched will be ignored. There is a general belief that one should always present the back of the hand to a strange dog. Working with dogs as I do in close contact with a great variety of self-styled dog lovers I find the efforts to carry out this exercise as amusing as it is unsuccessful.

Perhaps the commonest of all mistakes which people make in approaching a strange dog (and that includes a new puppy) is to stare at it. The only animal which likes its friends to look it 'straight in the eye' is the human being. Other animals do this only if they are afraid of each other or are about to attack. Watch two dogs meeting. If they look straight at each other you can expect a fight but if they approach shoulder to shoulder and walk stiffly round and round each other they will end up on friendly terms; so never stare at a new puppy when you are trying to get on friendly terms.

Now you are out in the garden with your pride and joy and you want him to come when called. He is probably sniffing around the gatepost or digging up the flower bed. Don't call him – for the simple and obvious reason that he won't come anyhow! An untrained puppy will do the thing which provides, or is likely to provide, the greatest pleasure at the time. Anyone who thinks that his voice is more attractive to a puppy than a hole in the ground or a smell on a gatepost has got the puppy's priorities wrong. Wait until the puppy appears to have nothing important to do and call it then. The best time is usually when he happens to be coming to you anyhow. Crouch down, hand extended, and call the puppy in a friendly persuasive tone. When he reaches you make a great fuss, fondle him and possibly offer a reward in the form of food. Do this several times when the puppy is sure to come and he will soon associate the sound of his name with the reward of food and/or petting. He will then have this association of ideas to strengthen the natural inclination to go to a friendly voice or hand. In most cases this combination will soon be strong enough to induce the puppy to leave the hole he is digging or the smell he is sniffing.

The mistake most people make is in never calling the puppy unless he is doing something they don't want him to do – which is usually something he *does* want to do. Every time you call a puppy and he obeys you (even if he happened to be coming anyhow) you have gone a step forward. Every time you call him and he disobeys you you have gone a step back. And if you persist in calling him when he is certain to disobey you, you will actually teach him *not* to come when called. Whatever you do, never, under any circumstances, scold or correct a dog in any way when it comes to you – no matter how much you feel like murdering it!

Now we have a puppy which comes to you in response to reward alone. But he will only do so if the reward is better than the alternative – and dog's lives, like ours, are made up of alternatives. A puppy will probably find food and petting more rewarding than aimlessly digging a hole or sniffing round a gatepost. But if the hole leads to a stinking old bone previously buried there or, when the dog is a bit older, a bitch in season has been around the gatepost, cooing voice, outstretched hand and pocketfuls of titbits may prove to be a poor alternative. We must then resort to correction as well as reward to build up the association we want. It should be noted that correction is only resorted to when reward has failed.

Our puppy is back in the same hole and you call him as before. But this is a much more interesting hole and, if the puppy responds at all, it is merely to look up as if saying 'Hang on a minute, I'm busy'. Here we have a situation where it is very easy to correct the puppy as he is doing the wrong thing and you should always take advantage of such opportunities. You have *asked* the puppy to come by calling his name in a nice friendly tone and he has refused. Call his name again, this time *telling* him to come in a very firm tone. It is possible that the puppy may respond to this change of tone. If so, change your tone of voice and whole attitude completely, and reward him with enthusiasm. If he does not respond pick up a handful of earth or small gravel and call him again even more harshly. If he does not respond this time throw the earth or gravel at him. As this 'hail' descends on him from heaven he will almost certainly get a fright and look round for a protector – that's you! Call him to you, make a great fuss of him and do all you can to console him in his misfortune. The object is to get him to associate the harsh tone of voice with something nasty out of the blue. He must not know that you threw it and, if you do it properly, it is almost certain that next time he hears that harsh tone he will anticipate another 'hailstorm' and rush to you for protection – which you must always provide.

    Never allow a puppy to run loose in a strange place until he will come to you every time you call him in the house or garden. Even then, you may find that when he sees another dog in the park he rushes off. I cannot over-emphasise the importance of nipping this habit in the bud and the best way for the novice is probably by using a check cord – about thirty feet of light cord attached to a dog's collar at one end with the other end in your hand. Let the puppy rush off and, as he nears the end of the cord call his name in a harsh tone. This time, instead of the handful of earth, the jerk on the check cord will provide the correction. He will probably do a somersault but don't worry. This method has been used by generations of gun dog trainers and I have never heard of a dog hurting himself. As he recovers from the jerk call him in a nice friendly tone and, when he reaches you, reward him lavishly. Never drag him to you. The line should be used as a means of correction when the dog tries to run away but you should encourage him to you by reward.

    This method of training should naturally never be

carried out until the dog is on a collar and lead and it is unlikely that a puppy will run after other dogs until he is about six months old. He will have to learn to go on a collar and lead before you take him out in public, and the place to teach him is not on the street or in the park but in his own garden or even indoors. Remember that a lead should never be regarded as a means of making a dog go with you but merely as a means of preventing him going too far away. Never put a collar and lead on a puppy until he will follow you without one.

There is a lot of argument about the best type of collar. Generally speaking, an ordinary buckled leather collar is as good as any for a puppy to start with. The puppy can be allowed to wear one and become quite familiar with it before the lead is put on. Start with a long lead and use it only to stop the puppy. Encourage him to come with you by rewarding him in the ways I have already described. Providing he will follow you without a lead (even if you do carry food in your pocket) he should soon follow you with one. It is more a question of familiarisation than actual training.

The usual problem is not how to get a puppy to go on a lead but how to stop him pulling once he has become familiar with it.

Here again this should be stopped before it becomes a habit, which is easier to prevent than to cure. It is important that when the puppy pulls you do not pull against him. Correct him for pulling with a sharp jerk on the lead and when he comes back to you in response, praise him well. Obviously you cannot jerk a dog on a short lead. For training a lead should be three or four feet long, pliable (we now use nylon web leads almost entirely), with a strong clip. If the puppy pulls, let the lead go suddenly and, before he has regained his balance, give him a sharp jerk. With a young puppy quite a small jerk will suffice, but it requires a considerable amount of skill and strength to cure an adult dog of pulling. There is little pleasure in taking out a dog which constantly pulls so, for your own sake as well as the dog's, don't let the habit develop.

If, in spite of your efforts, the puppy is pulling by the

time he is six months old I would suggest taking him to a local training class. I have mixed feelings about training classes where one often finds the blind leading the blind – not very successfully either! I get a great many cries for help from dog owners and almost all of them have already attended training classes! Some of the advice given by self-styled experts is quite frightening. I have met many sensitive dogs with temperaments completely ruined by classes.

On the other hand I know many dogs and owners who have benefited beyond belief. Like many other successful trainers, I started by going to classes. It really all depends on the instructor who in this country (not in America) gives his services free. Unfortunately free advice is often worth just what it costs. My advice is to go along to a training class (the Kennel Club will give you a list of those in your area) without your dog and see whether dogs which have been attending for some time behave in the way you want your dog to behave.

You now have a puppy which is clean in the house, comes when you call it (and stays with you) and walks on a loose lead. The other important exercise to make him a pleasure rather than a nuisance is that he stays where he is told without bringing complaints from the neighbours. Here we must go right back to the beginning with the puppy in the play pen. If, when you leave him, he cries to get out and you take him out you will be rewarding him for crying. It is incredible how quickly a young puppy will learn that whenever it wants attention all it has to do is howl. The longer you stay with a puppy coddling and consoling him the longer he will whine or howl when you leave him. If you go away and leave him alone he will probably howl for a bit and then settle down and go to sleep. A puppy accustomed from the start to being left alone in his play pen is unlikely to create any problems when you come to leave him in the car or any other strange place.

If he does persist in howling or barking when left alone, put him in his pen or just shut him in a room and go away. Stop when you get out of sight and wait for the noise to start. When it does, go back quietly. The puppy won't hear you when he is making a noise but he will whenever he stops, so you must stop and wait until he starts again. The idea is to get right up to the door while he is actually making a noise, then open it suddenly (which will surprise him anyhow) grab hold of him and scold him severely. Now start all over again, and if he makes a noise repeat the whole process. It is unlikely that he will make a noise this time so wait a few moments (don't tempt Providence by waiting too long) and go back to him again. This time make a great fuss to reward him for being quiet.

The usual mistake people make is unintentionally rewarding the dog for making a noise. The say 'Now, now, be a good boy. Don't make a noise', or 'It's all right, Mummy's here. No need to cry about it', and they say it all in the most soothing and rewarding tone possible. Having been rewarded by tone of voice (probably by gentle stroking too) for barking or whining the dog naturally does it again, and again, and again for as long as he is rewarded. It is interesting to note that bad tempered owners never have problems of this sort. They don't wonder what to do or read books on the subject. The dog irritates them by making a noise and, as it is actually barking, is told in no uncertain terms to 'Shut up'. If it doesn't, it gets a hefty clout on the ear and next time it hears 'Shut up' it shuts up! That is not how I train dogs or believe that dogs should be trained but it is effective.

Your pup should now be clean in the house, come when

called (at any time and in any place) and be quiet when left on his own. And that is more than can be said for many of the dogs working in the Obedience Championships at Crufts! If you do aspire to more advanced training (and I hope some of my readers will) there are several books on the subject and plenty of people willing to offer advice.

## JOHN HOLMES

An animal man if ever there was one, John Holmes was born and brought up on a farm in Scotland, and is the son of a famous breeder and exhibitor of Clydesdale horses and a judge of horses and cattle. As a boy he kept terriers who earned their keep by keeping the farm free of vermin. As an encore the terrier team entertained the farm workers and locals with a variety of party tricks. Later he graduated to training sheep- and cattle-dogs, using them for real work; he drove sheep ten miles to Perth market once a week, summer and winter, for a number of years.

He bought his first Corgi, Nippy of Drumharrow, in 1933 for two guineas, and later owned many famous Corgis. Mr Holmes took up obedience training after the war and in 1950 won the Junior Stakes at the ASPADS Trials; he then started training difficult and disobedient dogs for other people, and in no time at all became a prominent figure with a nationwide reputation.

In his own words, at this point he really began to learn about dogs and, more important, dog people. He ran dog training classes at Henley on Thames, and among other successes the instructor married his 'star pupil'. Together, Mr and Mrs Holmes built up a team of dogs who gave displays all over the British Isles – a mongrel from the team started his film career in 'Knave of Hearts'. This was quickly followed by a television series of dog programmes, 'Your Dog and Mine', for which John supplied the performers. Since then he has handled all sorts of other animals, including rats, on hundreds of films, television plays and commercials, and has appeared in numerous documentaries and discussion programmes on television. His film, 'A Tale of Two Puppies', was networked over all regions around Christmas 1970, and he has also made a seven-episode series for Southern Television called 'Training the Family Dog' based on his book *The Family Dog* (now in its fifth edition). Other books by John Holmes include *The Farmer's Dog* (about training sheep- and cattle-dogs) and *Obedience Training for Dogs*.

J.C.

# 6 Breeding

BY BETTY PENN-BULL

There is an old theory that every bitch should have a litter, but there seems to be no evidence to support this, so unless there is a definite desire to breed, the certainty of placing the resulting puppies satisfactorily, and the ability to provide the necessary care and attention, it is not advisable to embark on mating a bitch.

My opinion is that a bitch is best bred from either regularly or not at all, and that the single, so-called 'therapeutic' litter may well unsettle her, awakening the maternal and breeding instincts which are then subsequently thwarted if she is not allowed further puppies.

I have known many maiden bitches which have lived healthy lives into ripe old age, and I do not advise anyone to mate a bitch unless the puppies are really wanted. Never do so 'for her sake' and risk bringing puppies into the world for which it may be impossible to find good and suitable homes.

There are new opinions these days in regard to spaying bitches, and this now seems to be more acceptable than it used to be. But it is important that a bitch is fully developed before this is done, and she should have had at least one season in order to have reached complete maturity. Guide Dogs For The Blind use spayed bitches almost without exception, and this has not been found to affect their disposition, health, well-being or ability to work adversely.

Small breeds are usually easily controlled when in season, but with the larger ones, or where premises are not completely secure from invasion by trespassing dogs, spaying is certainly preferable to mis-mating and a subsequent unwanted litter.

Bitches used for breeding should conform to certain standards physically and mentally, and those falling short of these requirements should be discarded. They should be sound and healthy, of good type and conformation, and free from structural, organic or hereditary defects. In addition they should be of good temperament; nervous or bad-tempered stock should not be bred from. People sometimes appear to have the wrong ideas about breeding and I have heard remarks like, 'She is so nervous and excitable, I think a litter will steady her'; 'She keeps getting skin trouble, I hope having puppies will help to clear it up'. I feel this argument should be in reverse. Are these dogs suitable to be bred from? Do we want half a dozen more with poor temperaments or with some physical disability? If the answer is that we do not, then the simple solution is not to breed from such stock, and they should be excluded from one's breeding programme. The possibility of benefiting the parent at the expense of the unborn young is a wrong concept.

Before being mated the bitch should be in top condition and perfect health. She should be well nourished on a properly balanced diet with ample protein, but it is preferable if she is a little on the lean side rather than slightly too fat.

Bitches normally come into season for the first time at about nine months of age, and thereafter at six monthly intervals. But there may be some variation in these times and this is not necessarily an indication of any abnormality. Small dogs in particular may have their first heat as young as seven or eight months of age, while larger ones may be a year old or even older. The cycle may vary too, and occasionally a bitch will go twelve months between seasons, while with some of the smaller breeds it may occur again after only four months' intervals. But if a bitch has three seasons in a year, one of these will not be fertile. Usually, after a litter the cycle adjusts and the times revert to the normal six months. When a bitch is due in season she should be tested each day with a swab of cotton wool pressed to the vulva to check for the first sign of colour. She can then be observed, and the pattern of her season noted.

As a rule, dogs tend to sniff around a bitch and show interest before the season actually starts, and this is often an indication that it is pending. But once the colour appears most dogs leave a bitch severely alone during the early period and I do not usually find it necessary to segregate her for at least six or seven days. After this time she must be carefully isolated.

Colour usually continues for about nine or ten days and then it gradually begins to fade, and by about twelve days, which is normally the height of the season, there is either just a pinkish tinge or it is practically colourless. As a rule the heat lasts for three weeks and the bitch must be kept isolated until the end of this period whether mated or not.

With some of the smaller breeds there is a more rapid cycle, the colour fades sooner and the bitch may be ready at eight or nine days, and the season completely over in fourteen or fifteen days. Some of the larger breeds may not be ready to mate until fourteen to sixteen days or even later, and their season may last twenty-four days, or occasionally even longer, so each bitch must be studied individually. It is important to note details of the first season as this can be helpful on subsequent occasions if a mating is intended.

With the smaller breeds the second season is a suitable time for mating, and this usually occurs at about fifteen months of age. But if a bitch is being shown, or it is not convenient, she can be left until later. It is advisable when possible to have her first litter by about three years of age while the frame is still elastic and has not hardened too much.

If a bitch is bred from regularly but has not been over-bred, I have known a number to continue having successful litters up to eight years of age. But it is important that she is maintained in good condition and receives the right care and attention.

It is not possible to generalise in regard to the frequency with which one can mate a bitch as each case must be assessed on its own merits.

As a rough guide the larger breeds which also tend to have larger litters may need a longer time between litters. With the smaller breeds one can often have two litters in succession and then miss a season without putting an undue strain on the bitch. But other factors come into account too, particularly the number of puppies produced and reared. If a bitch had seven or eight and reared all I would rest her a year before the next litter. But if she had only three or four I would consider mating her at her next heat. This would apply during the prime of her life, between two and six years old, but after six years of age I would not breed from her more than once a year.

Other factors must be considered too, such as her general health, condition and activity and whether she is an easy whelper. Some dogs of seven are like four-year-olds, and others are like ten-year-olds, so all these matters must be taken into account.

Arrangements should be made well in advance with the owner of the selected stud dog, and it is customary for her to visit him. A provisional date should be fixed as soon as she starts in season which can be varied later if necessary.

If the bitch is sent by rail she should be despatched two or three days before the height of her season and in consultation with the owner of the dog. She should be sent in a secure and comfortable box, properly labelled and with careful arrangements for her collection.

If she is taken personally which is preferable whenever possible, it is important the timing is correct to ensure maximum prospects of a successful outcome, and this entails the careful assessment of the vital factors of the timing, colour and her reactions. On arrival the bitch should be allowed a free run to relieve herself, to stretch her legs and to settle down a little after her journey, before being introduced to the dog. The actual mating procedure is dealt with under the section concerned with the stud dog.

After mating, the bitch must be kept segregated until the completion of her season, and she can then resume her normal life.

*Care of the Bitch In Whelp*
The bitch in whelp should be well cared for, but not coddled. For the first few weeks she may carry on with her ordinary routine providing this does not entail any excessive exertion. But she will be all the better for plenty of freedom

and exercise, interspersed with adequate rest periods. She should not be allowed to get cold or wet, and should also be protected from excessive heat.

During the last few weeks several short walks are preferable to one long one, but she should be encouraged to keep active with gentle exercise until the end, although avoiding anything unduly strenuous. She should have as much liberty as possible and should not be closely confined except for minimal periods.

Feeding the in-whelp bitch may vary to some degree. With the small breeds, and with some which are not always easy whelpers, great care must be taken not to over-feed, and the aim is to produce small, strong puppies at birth, as larger ones may well be the cause of trouble at whelping time.

I feed as usual for the first six weeks, but I do ensure there is an ample meat ration, plus a limited amount of biscuit and raw or cooked vegetables. I give two equal meals for the last three weeks, increasing the meat allowance but decreasing the starch to a minimum. I give cod liver oil daily, but this is the only additive my bitches in whelp receive as they are a breed which are not always easy whelpers, so I ration them carefully. I do not add calcium or bone meal, or give milk or eggs or other extras.

But with many other breeds, and particularly the larger ones, it will be advisable to step up the rations after mating, and probably to provide various additives too, as this particular problem of whelping does not apply in all cases.

The big breeds usually have larger litters and the puppies are proportionately smaller at birth in relation to the size of the dam. So within certain limits the breeder must be guided by the needs of the individual bitch in deciding on the correct policy.

I give a small teaspoonful of liquid paraffin daily during the last week. I also give the bitch a thorough grooming and overhaul several days before the litter is due. This consists of a good brushing and combing into every corner. She is then sponged over with a cloth wrung out in weak Dettol and warm water, paying particular attention to the feet, under the body, the head, between the legs and under the tail. The anal gland is checked and cleared if necessary. The eyes and ears are examined and treated if required, and the mouth and teeth are inspected and cleaned if necessary.

Any excessive hair round feet, tummy and other parts may be tidied up if desired, but although I have a breed with furnishings I do not remove them from my bitches. Some breeders do, and this is a matter for the individual to decide.

*The Whelping Quarters*
The bitch should be introduced to the place where she is to whelp some days before the event, so she feels settled and relaxed there. This should be a quiet room or building, or an enclosed pen where she has privacy and is not worried by other dogs or by children or strangers.

The whelping box should be placed here, and it should be roomy enough for her to lie full length and still allow a margin of space beyond this. It should be raised on low slats to allow air to circulate beneath the base. There should be a removable board to slot into the front, but this should be taken out before whelping to avoid any risk of injury when the bitch goes in and out of the box. The sides of the box should be high enough to protect the bitch and puppies from draughts and a removable lid is an advantage.

A crush barrier should be provided which can be inserted into the box, with a clearance of two or more inches from the ground, and two or more inches from the sides of the box, according to the size of the dog, to avoid the possibility of the puppies being pressed behind the dam, and perhaps suffocated. This is similar to the pig-rail used for farrowing sows and provides a safe alley-way while the puppies are small. This barrier should not be put into position until after the bitch has finished whelping and it can be removed when the puppies are two or three weeks old, when they require more room and will be stronger.

I use an infra-red lamp for my litters and this is positioned across one corner of the box, so there is a warm spot for the puppies, but the opposite corner is cool if the dam prefers to lie there.

My whelping box has vinyl on the floor and this is then covered with several layers of newspaper and finally a thick blanket for the bitch and litter.

*The Whelping*
Bitches carry their young for sixty-three days, but this is subject to some variation. It is quite usual for a bitch to whelp three days early, while some of the smaller breeds may have their puppies five days before time. Puppies born more than five days early have a limited chance of survival. Some bitches may go overtime, but if this extends more than two or three days there is some cause for concern and there may be trouble ahead.

The first indication that whelping may be imminent is a drop in temperature which will fall below 100° (normal temperature in the dog is 101·4°). This may occur two or three days before the actual whelping, but when the temperature drops to 98° or 97° the whelping will generally occur within twenty-four hours.

The preliminary signs are restlessness, trembling, yawning, panting, bed-making, and possibly vomiting. Food is usually refused, and there is often a desire to pass water frequently.

All these symptoms may be present, or only some, and they may last for some hours, or even intermittently for a full day or more. But the whelping as such does not really commence until the contractions begin, so until that time it is a matter of waiting for further developments.

If there is a rise in temperature or a black or green discharge, trouble is indicated and veterinary advice must be sought without delay.

But if all appears normal do not interfere unnecessarily, but allow the bitch the opportunity to whelp. Some are slower than others, and it sometimes pays to be patient providing there are no abnormal symptoms.

Many bitches like the comfort of their owner's presence at this time, and a reassuring word and a little fondling will encourage them. Firm, but gentle stroking down the back is sometimes helpful in stimulating the contractions.

The bitch should not be fussed or agitated and the owner

should remain calm and cheerful. The bitch can be offered glucose and milk or glucose and water from time to time, or she may be given a little brandy or whisky, but she should not have any solid food during whelping as this may cause vomiting.

The first puppy may appear quite quickly once the contractions start, or it may not come for two or three hours, or even more in some cases, as some bitches are much slower than others.

It is sometimes difficult to decide at what stage assistance should be given, and if an owner is a complete novice it is helpful to have an experienced breeder available who can advise in the event of any queries or difficulties or suggest when professional help is necessary.

The puppy should arrive head first, contained in its sac and with the afterbirth attached, and the dam should quickly release the puppy, cleaning it thoroughly and eating the afterbirth. But some bitches, particularly maidens, are slow at freeing the puppy's head, and in this case the breeder must do so without delay or fluid will get into the puppy's lungs and this may be fatal. The bitch should then be encouraged to lick and massage the puppy. If it is slow in breathing it should be rubbed and shaken and any fluid drawn from the nose and mouth; warmth is very important in helping to revive it.

The flat-nosed breeds are not usually able to attend to their newly-born whelps, and the attendant must be prepared to assist them by removing the puppy from the bag and severing the cord. The puppy should then be offered to the dam for her to clean and lick. If several puppies are born in rapid succession it may be advisable to remove some of the earlier ones temporarily and place them in a warm box away from the dam until the whelping is completed so that the newer arrivals can receive more attention, and the earlier ones do not get cold and neglected. But if this upsets the dam they must be left with her and endeavours made to keep them warm and dry. I use thick newspapers for the whelping and old sacks or blankets, and I put in more paper or old towels as we go along, to try and keep the bed as clean and dry as possible.

When the whelping is finished one person should take the bitch out to make herself comfortable. Meanwhile, a second person should gently lift out the puppies, then remove the soiled bedding, wipe round the box and put in fresh paper and a clean blanket. The anti-crush frame should then be inserted, the front board slotted in and the puppies replaced. The dam should then be allowed back, to find everything ship-shape, thus avoiding her being agitated by a lot of commotion going on around her.

She should be offered a warm drink and then left quietly to rest for a few hours, although it is generally wise to keep an unobtrusive eye on her to make sure all is well. I leave a small light for the first few days as I prefer a dull emitter lamp over the bed.

*Post-Natal Care and Feeding*
For the first few days after whelping it is important to check the bitch's mammary glands regularly. Run the hands lightly over all her teats and these should be soft and yielding. If one or more are hard and congested this indicates the puppies are not suckling from these, and this may result in milk fever or an abcess, so steps must be taken immediately to alleviate the condition.

The trouble is more likely to occur with small litters when the puppies are obtaining adequate milk supplies without drawing on all the teats. Those most likely to be affected are the back ones which often carry heavy milk yields, and to a lesser extent the front ones may also be affected. The middle breasts do not seem as likely to be involved and are usually those most readily drawn on by the puppies.

As soon as the condition is diagnosed the affected breast should be gently massaged and softened with warm poultices to ease the pressure. Then some of the milk should be drawn off, and when it is flowing freely one of the strongest puppies should be placed on the teat and encouraged to suck. When he has had his fill he should be replaced by another until the breast is clear.

There may be no further trouble once it is soft and pliable, and the puppies may now use it normally. But it

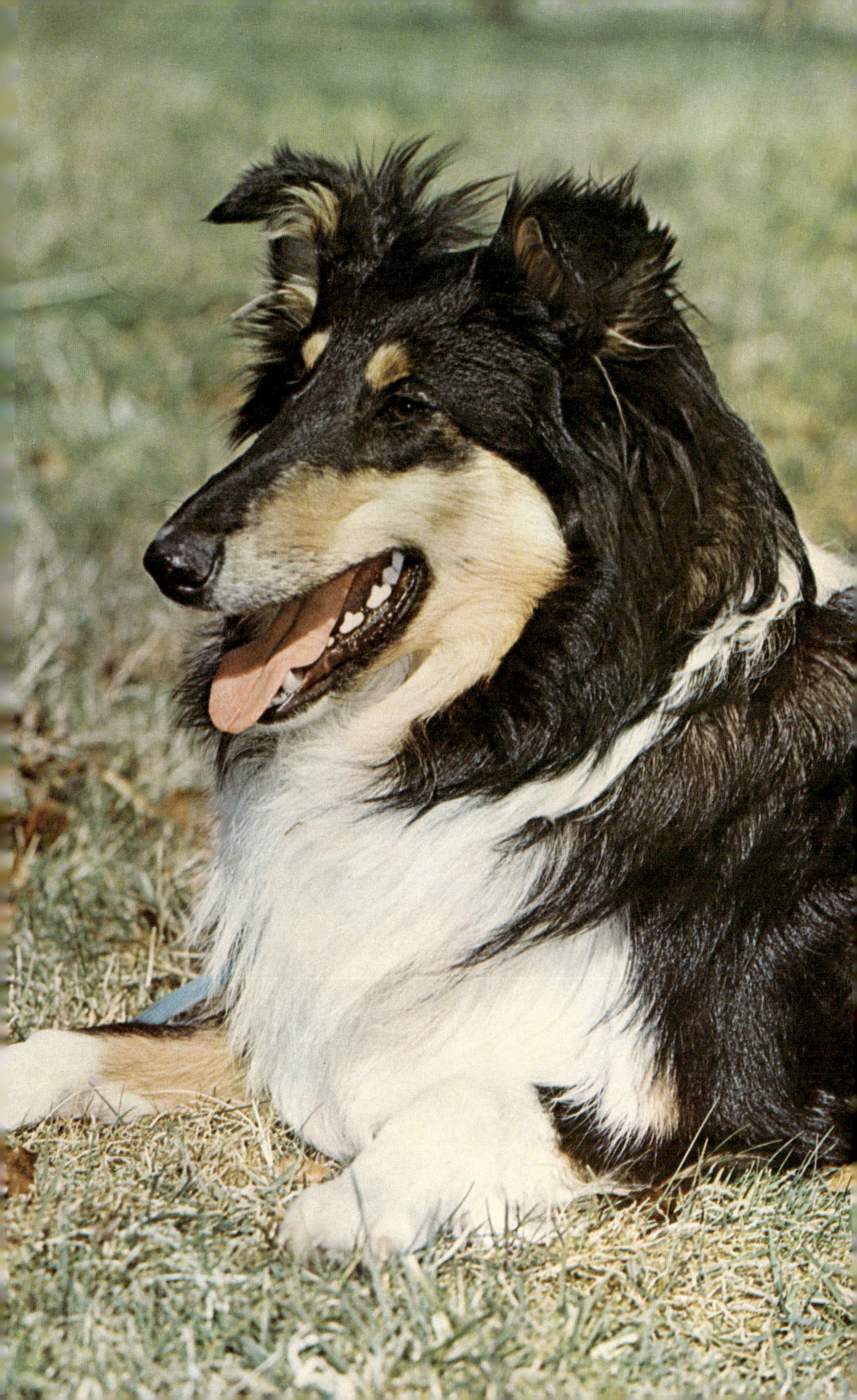

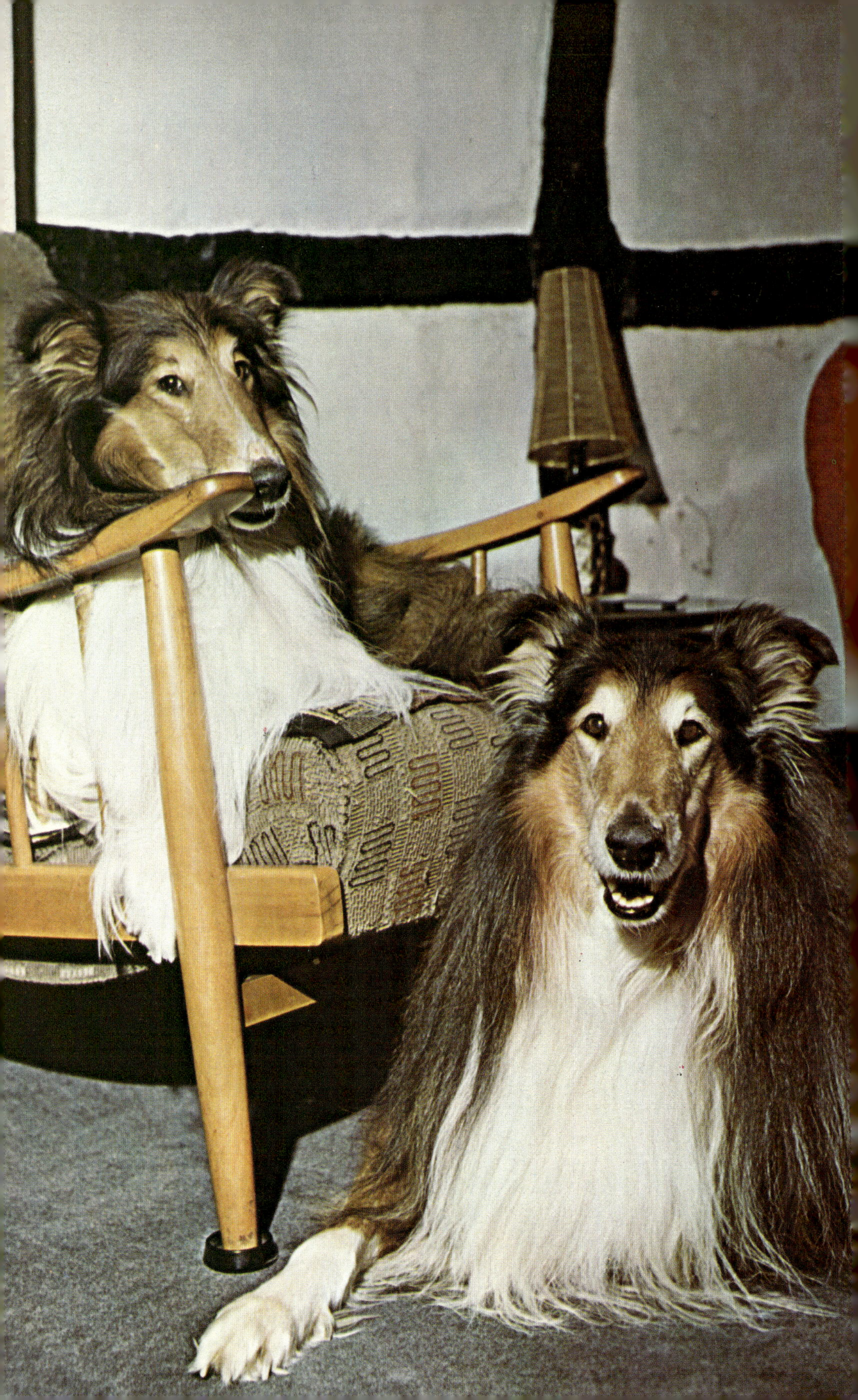

must be watched and the treatment repeated if necessary. Once a gland becomes really congested and hard the puppies will avoid it as they are unable to draw the milk from it in this condition, so it is essential to get the milk flowing to avert any possible complications. The dam must also be kept under careful observation to ensure there are no complications as an aftermath of the whelping. Any rise in temperature, refusal of food, vomiting, unhealthy discharge, or diarrhoea should alert the breeder.

There may be retention of a puppy and if this is dead professional help must be summoned without delay; or perhaps the bitch has failed to pass one or more of the afterbirths, in which case an injection to encourage this may be called for, or antibiotics may be necessary. So it is essential to seek advice immediately if any abnormal symptoms such as these should occur.

If there is no infection and no complications, the bitch will usually be happy and relaxed after the birth, and ready to take nourishment, so any signs of discomfort or distress should cause the breeder to suspect something to be wrong, and he should therefore take the necessary steps to obtain advice or help should any untoward symptoms manifest themselves.

Once the puppies are safely born the bitch should be fed generously and this applies to nursing mothers of all breeds as suckling puppies imposes a great strain on the dam.

I give fluid feeds only for the first twenty-four hours. Then for the next twenty-four hours I add semi-solids such as fish, minced meat and eggs. If all is going normally I then gradually revert to ordinary food, simultaneously increasing the quantity given. From about a week after whelping until the puppies are weaned the dam will be fed lavishly with plenty of flesh (raw meat, stewed beef, ox-cheek, offal, sheep's head, paunch, fish, etc.), milk feeds of various kinds, eggs, broth, wholemeal food and vegetables. She also has calcium and cod liver oil, or similar additives.

If the litter is a large one I give three meat feeds and two milk meals during this period. If there are only a few puppies less food will be required, but this must be judged by the bitch's and the puppies' condition and her milk supply. Leave fresh water always available as nursing mothers require ample liquids.

*Weaning the Litter*
I like to start weaning puppies early to lessen the strain on the dam, and also to make this as gradual a process as possible. Scraped raw beef and enriched milk can be offered at the third week, and at four weeks puppies can be having two small feeds of each of these each day. Other items are then introduced gradually: cooked meat of various kinds, fish, and a variety of milk feeds, plus fine puppy meal or crumbled wholemeal bread. I also add cod-liver oil and calcium or their equivalents daily.

At five weeks mine have five meals a day, three of meat and two milk meals and I continue this until they are eight or ten weeks old. At five weeks I consider puppies to be fully weaned, but the dam is still allowed to visit them if she wishes to, but is never compelled to be with them. In fact from the time of the birth the dam is always free to get out of the box and away from the puppies if she wishes to do so.

*Worming and Other Matters*
Puppies should be wormed at least twice before sale, and they should not go to their new homes younger than eight weeks old. They should always be accompanied by a diet chart and instructions as to correct care and routine should also be given to the new owner.

Some breeds seem especially subject to worms despite every possible precaution. With my breed I find it necessary to dose at about three weeks old and again ten days later, with perhaps a third worming at about eight weeks old. But other breeds appear to be less susceptible, and it may be possible to defer the first worming until five or six weeks old, followed by a second dose a week or so later. One point I have observed is that puppies from maiden or young bitches seem to be much more liable to heavy worm infestation, and that as the dams grow older their progeny do not seem to be affected to the same degree.

Indications of worm infestation in young puppies are

coat standing on end, hard and distended stomach, unhealthy motions, passing jelly or mucus, and a lack of weight gain. These symptoms may develop at a very early age and it is then advisable to dose without delay. The modern preparations are safe and effective and no fasting is required, and I have found no risk or danger involved in the treatment. Worming does not give puppies permanent immunity but they should remain clear for some weeks, although it may be advisable to repeat the treatment when they are about four months old, and subsequently as and when it appears necessary.

A further point is to keep puppies' nails short and they should be clipped each week to prevent them scratching the dam or catching in the bedding.

If tails must be docked and dew-claws cut these should be done a few days after birth. It is not a difficult job, but it is advisable for the novice to obtain the help of an experienced person to undertake this task. Care should be taken that tails are docked to the correct length as this varies for different breeds.

*Some Aspects Concerning Dogs*

Only suitable males should be used for breeding, and in addition to the same general requirements of good health and temperament which apply to bitches, the standards required regarding type and quality should, if possible, be even higher. Fewer males are required in a breeding programme, so the elimination process must be even more stringent. With working dogs the same rules of strict selection should also apply.

Those dogs which do not measure up to the desired standard should not be used at stud, and it is a mistaken conviction to assume that every dog should be mated. Apart from other considerations this would not be practical, for numbers would get completely out of control in the dog population, with a rapid increase in 'also-rans' and unwanted puppies.

If a dog is used regularly at stud he generally falls into a pattern of life and does not worry unless a bitch is ready for mating. But a dog which is used only once or twice during his life tends to become awakened but not satisfied, and may well be more frustrated than if not used at all.

Most males settle down after puberty and do not worry unduly, but some breeds or individuals tend to be more highly sexed than others, and if a dog becomes an embarrassment the question of castration should be considered. This course is not generally necessary but in extreme cases it may be the best solution. The worried owner of an over-sexed dog may feel that if only he were mated it would calm him, but it will not generally solve any problems and as already suggested the condition will probably be aggravated.

So my advice is that you should accept that your dog will fall into one of three categories: firstly, top dogs to be used for breeding, secondly, other dogs which are kept for various purposes – as companions, as guards or for work. These dogs to remain entire, but not used at stud, and thirdly, dogs which are not suitable for breeding, but which are difficult and where castration may be advisable.

*Care of the Stud Dog*
A dog used regularly at stud must be kept in good condition, fit, hard and active. He should not be over-weight, but must be generously fed with a good proportion of protein in his diet. The frequency with which a dog may be used will vary according to a number of factors. Perhaps as a rough guide, the smaller and medium breeds might average two matings a week during the dog's prime when between two and six years old, and this should not tax him unduly. With younger dogs, under two years old, perhaps once a week would be wiser, and the same would apply to those over six years of age. But such suggestions are subject to variation and must be elastic. I have known of dogs used much more frequently without apparent ill effects. With the bigger breeds it would not generally be advisable to use them as frequently as the smaller ones, but the question does not generally arise since they are not usually bred on a large scale in any case.

External considerations of management, handling, condition and the individual dog's potency, etc., must all play their part. If a dog is well cared for and is healthy and virile he may retain his fertility until he is in his 'teens; but this is unusual and not many dogs are still useful at stud after nine or ten years of age.

If a dog mates quickly and easily he can be used much more frequently than another, which requires several attempts to achieve a mating. The latter can lose more energy over one unsuccessful effort than the former would do in mating two or three bitches.

If a dog mates without trouble he will not be exhausted and will be as fit as before; after a little rest he will be ready to enjoy his food and be back to normal. If well managed a dog can be in regular use at stud and still keep in top condition for the show ring.

But conversely, the dog which steams about for prolonged periods, trying ineffectively until he is exhausted, panting and wild-eyed, and with his heart racing, will be far more spent. He is frustrated and upset and probably will not eat or rest, and these sessions if embarked on frequently will soon take their toll of a dog's condition.

*The Mating*
It is best to start a dog at stud when young as this is more likely to ensure an easy mating, and this could be at about ten months to a year old for a small dog and perhaps eighteen months or so for a large one.

It is preferable to commence a maiden dog with a steady and experienced brood bitch, as a nervy or snappy one can upset a youngster. A small, empty, enclosed area is usually best for the mating, where the dogs are not distracted, and where there are no obstructions to impede matters or to make the dogs inaccessible if help is necessary.

Usually two people should be present, one to concentrate on the dog and the other on the bitch. But sometimes with big powerful dogs or those which are obstreperous, extra help may be required to steady the animals.

The bitch should be on the lead so she is under control, but she should be allowed free play to encourage the dog, and meanwhile the dog should be allowed to make advances and to gain confidence. The bitch must be the focal point and the handlers should remain background figures. Encouragement and praise may be offered, but these should be given quietly so as not to divert the dog's main interest from the bitch.

On no account should the dog be scolded or curbed, and no anger or irritation should ever be apparent during a mating or potential mating. If the bitch is aggressive she must be controlled, but this must be done by calming and soothing her, and by firm handling, or if necessary by muzzling her, and on no account by roughness or violent actions.

It is most important that matings are carried out in a tranquil atmosphere so a dog retains his confidence. If he is subjected to harshness or to inconsistent treatment, or is frightened or upset in any way, he may become an unreliable stud dog, easily discouraged, and reluctant to co-operate with his handler.

It is my considered opinion that many potentially valuable stud dogs are lost to their breeds, or have restricted opportunities because of mishandling, so it is very important to approach the situation sympathetically.

Sometimes a bitch may suffer from a stricture which makes the mating difficult, or even impossible, so if the dog appears to be striking correctly but does not achieve a 'tie', the bitch should be examined to test if the passage is clear. The small finger, first sterilised and then covered with a little petroleum jelly as a lubricant, should be gently inserted into the passage.

If the way is clear the finger will slip in easily, but if an obstruction is felt it will be necessary to stretch this, or break it down, to enable the dog to penetrate. This can generally be done by easing the finger in with a screwing action, gently pressing and twisting and working it to and fro. The stricture may consist of a strip of skin across the passage which will require stretching or breaking down, or it may be a thickened band ringing the passage which will need enlarging to allow a way through. If this treatment is carried out slowly and carefully it does not upset the bitch, but on no account must it be done roughly.

When the bitch shows signs of being prepared to accept

the dog, by turning her tail, and if the dog tries to mount her, the handlers should be ready to assist if required. The one assigned to the bitch should steady her and should be prepared to hold her firmly with both hands should she jerk as the dog is mating her. Meanwhile, the other handler should be watching the dog, ready if necessary to give him some support if he shows signs of slipping away from the bitch before he has effected the mating. Once he is mated he should be kept on the bitch's back for a minute or two before being allowed to turn, as if not fully 'locked' he may come away if he turns too quickly.

With some of the smaller dogs it is customary not to turn them, but they are held on the bitch's back until the completion of the tie. With some of the larger ones it is usual to lower the dog beside the bitch as this seems more comfortable for many big dogs. But most make a complete turn and remain back to back during the mating, and this is the normal position. The length of the tie may vary from five or ten minutes to half an hour or more, but its duration has no relation to the results.

As they separate after mating I usually raise the bitch's hindquarters and gently tap the vulva which stimulates the contraction of the vaginal muscles. As the dogs part there is sometimes quite a back flow of fluid from the bitch, and I try and avert this as far as possible. Only a small amount of semen is required to fertilise the bitch but there is nothing to lose by taking what precautions one can!

If everything is normal with a satisfactory tie, one mating should be sufficient. But if there are any unsatisfactory aspects, such as the bitch coming into colour again, causing doubts as to the correct timing, if the tie was not a good one, or if perhaps she has a history as an unreliable breeder, then it may be wise to have a second mating.

If a bitch is difficult to get into whelp it is worth trying several spaced matings at three or four day intervals. Try the first one as early as possible, perhaps at seven or eight days; a second one at the normal time of perhaps eleven or twelve days, and another as late as possible, perhaps at fifteen or sixteen days. I have known bitches which do not follow the regular pattern, and which may require mating very early or very late to ensure conception, and this condition may be difficult to recognise and is only discovered and corrected by trial and error. But if a bitch is difficult to get into whelp it is worth trying varying the timing to endeavour to catch her at her most fertile period.

Sometimes there is a difference in height between the animals and it may be necessary to adjust this with a low platform. Usually it is the dog who requires raising, and a board (if necessary on blocks) may be used, preferably covered with a sack or a piece of carpet to give purchase.

Some breeders prefer to mate the smaller dogs on a bench or table and the dog soon becomes accustomed to this. Personally I prefer to mate them on the floor as I find it a natural sequence from the preliminary flirting, but this is an optional decision.

The bitch should be brought to the stud dog when she is ready for mating, and every effort should then be made to effect this. This is particularly necessary if a dog is young and valuable and likely to be in much demand at stud, for it is important to ensure he does not waste his energy and that he is not disappointed, which may undermine his confidence and determination. If a dog is brought in and out to a bitch which may or may not be ready, and if he is tried repeatedly and unsuccessfully, these abortive attempts can be most damaging to his future career at stud. Whereas if he is only introduced to bitches ready for mating and is given correct assistance, culminating in a successful outcome, he is likely to be fully co-operative and ready to tackle even the most difficult bitch, and he should become virtually one hundred per cent reliable.

It is most important that the bitch is never allowed to bite the dog, and this is even more vital with a youngster. If a dog is roughly treated by a bitch in his early days, this may affect him to the extent that he refuses to go near any other bitch which even growls, so the handler of the bitch must keep her under control and be sure that this does not happen.

If a young dog mounts the bitch incorrectly he must not be checked or restrained in any way but the bitch should be manoeuvred around towards him, and he should still be praised and encouraged. To check him would not imply 'Don't do it at that end – do it at this end' – it would simply mean 'Don't do that'.

I once had the greatest difficulty in handling a young dog whose owner had been 'training' him by giving him a slap every time he tried to mount the bitch at the wrong angle, at the same time scolding him and telling him what a silly dog he was, and that was not the right way to do it. Eventually I had to send her right away, out of his sight and sound as he was thoroughly bewildered by her apparently wanting him to mate the bitch and then giving him a smack when he tried to do so.

Sometimes a dog is shy and very reluctant to try to mate a bitch if people are near, but he does eventually succeed when running with her and while both are free. In this event it is wise to go quietly towards them once they are mated and to hold the dog gently, stroking and praising him quietly, and making relaxed contact, so he becomes accustomed to human proximity in these circumstances, and he may thus be willing to accept help on a subsequent occasion if the necessity arises.

Dogs running together may mate naturally sometimes, but sooner or later there will be problems and it may not be possible for the dog to effect the mating without some assistance. Either there may be a big difference in size between the animals which will require adjustment, or the bitch may jerk away at the crucial moment and require steadying. So unless the dog will accept human help, there will come a time when he may fail, so it is important for the breeder to accustom him to being handled.

After the mating the bitch should be shut away quietly for a rest before she is exercised or travels, and I try to avoid her passing water too soon. The dog too, should be put in his bed to relax and unwind for a period, and he should not be returned among other dogs for some time until he has completely settled down, when he can resume his normal life. If he is returned too quickly among other males this may create tension and such mishandling may well precipitate friction.

*Final Hints on Management*

I have kept stud dogs for many years, and I do not consider that they should be treated any differently from other dogs in their ordinary life, and my experience is that if they are treated normally they will respond normally.

But there are certain aspects which require careful management, and it is important not to inflame possible latent jealousy by allowing situations involving tension to occur.

Well before a bitch reaches the height of her season she must be removed and kept completely away from all stud dogs. If several dogs are running together and are able to see, or sniff, a bitch in season this will understandably cause friction, and possibly aggression and trouble.

I always run my dogs together, and have had as many as six or seven or more mature males mixing freely with each other and an equal number of bitches, all happy and friendly together, and I think when this can be managed dogs are much more contented and well adjusted.

It is sometimes considered that a stud dog must not mix with bitches or he will not mate them, but this has not been my experience, and I have had many very successful stud dogs who have lived as family pack dogs.

But although stud dogs may run together under supervision and in open areas, they should never be confined in small enclosures without somebody in attendance.

Young males of the same age which grow up together may not agree well when mature, as neither may be willing to accept the dominance of the other. But I have found if I grow on one new youngster at a time there is not this problem, as he automatically falls into his position as the junior member of the pack, and is thus integrated into the group. The next new addition to follow on falls into line under him and so on.

But I must add that I would never introduce a new adult male into an established pack and I doubt if this would be acceptable among many stud dogs. Some would mix readily on neutral ground, but they would not willingly accept a strange dog into their home surroundings.

## BETTY PENN-BULL

I cannot think of anyone in the world of dogs more capable of writing on the subject of breeding stock than Miss Betty Penn-Bull. Since she can remember Betty has always been immensely interested in dogs. Her literary background enables her to pass on her knowledge in an extremely readable way. Miss Penn-Bull's over-riding desire as a child was to own a dog, but she was never allowed one. Her ambition as a youngster was to make a career with dogs but this too received no support from her family and without any backing she proudly secured her first job aged seventeen. Betty was not able to count on any paid training. It included helping in the house to compensate for lack of experience. After eight kennel jobs gaining experience and having managed to save £35 to start her own kennels, she was fortunate in finding a stable for the equivalent of 25p per week. Single-handed and making every penny count, with trimming, puppy sales, breeding and the use of stud dogs, Miss Penn-Bull built up a strain of Kennelgarth Scottish Terriers who are second to none in the breed here in Britain and anywhere in the world where pedigree dogs are known. Miss Penn-Bull has, since these early days, never been away from dogs and dog shows. She has owned seventeen British champions and bred nine. Betty's home-bred Scottish Terrier Champion Kennelgarth Viking is the greatest top sire ever known, creating a record by siring twenty-three British champions.

J.C.

# 7 Common Illnesses, Recognition and Treatment BY MICHAEL STOCKMAN

It is not intended that this chapter should do anything other than describe what a healthy dog should look like and what steps should be taken if any definite change in that state of health should appear. It must be stressed that your veterinary surgeon is there to be consulted on any occasion where the trouble is outside the scope of your own capabilities and delay in obtaining professional advice may result in a worsening of symptoms and a more serious illness arising.

Before one can decide whether or not a dog is ill, it is first necessary to know the classic signs of health. In brief terms these are as follows:

    *a* Bright, clear eyes.
    *b* A healthy shining coat.
    *c* A readiness for exercise.
    *d* A good appetite.
    *e* The passage of normal quantities of urine and droppings of normal consistency and colour.

Against this may be listed the signs of abnormality:

    *a* Dullness of either eyes or coat.
    *b* Lethargy.
    *c* Lack of appetite.
    *d* Excessive thirst.
    *e* Excessive scratching.
    *f* Vomiting, diarrhoea and excessive urination.

It is obviously impossible in a single chapter to deal with any but a few of the main problems associated with disease and this I intend to do in alphabetical series.

### Accidents

These are usually associated with a painful collision with a car or vehicle, but may be the result of being kicked by a horse. Another accident is the scalded or burnt dog. All these should be examined by your veterinary surgeon as soon as possible and if it is necessary to move a heavy dog it is often possible to carry him on a large blanket. This will not only make the problem of weight much easier to cope with but will also keep the injured animal warm and help to guard against shock. While on the subject of accidents, it is well to mention that the dog in pain may well react to human attempts to assist by biting. That the helping hand may be the one that normally feeds him is no guarantee of immunity, so approach the injured dog with care. If possible apply a stout leather collar and hold on to it while moving or examining the patient.

*Allergies*
Many proteins can give rise to allergic reactions which manifest themselves in general by swellings appearing in the skin especially round the face. These symptoms are often referred to under the name of 'nettle-rash' and in most cases disappear as quickly as they arise, usually without treatment. Occasionally it is necessary to give an injection of an anti-histamine drug to counteract the histamine which has caused the allergy.

The cause may be something the dog has eaten, a sting from a bee or wasp or even a vaccine injection. Whatever the reason it is possible that more serious symptoms may arise as a result of the allergic reaction taking place in the lining of the stomach or intestine giving rise to vomiting, diarrhoea or dysentery with passage of blood with loose faeces. Reactions may also take place in the respiratory system producing signs of asthma-type breathing. Both these latter conditions are extremely serious and need very urgent attention from the veterinary surgeon. It cannot be too often stressed that when some urgent condition is apparent it is normally much better to put the patient in the car and drive straight to the nearest surgery rather than waiting for a veterinary surgeon to be contacted on the phone and directed to you. With the advent of multi-man practices running modern hospitals, all the necessary equipment is there to deal with an acute emergency.

*Anal Glands*
These are two secretory sacs lying just below and to either side of the anal opening. They produce a vile-smelling

protective secretion which in the wild dog presumably acted as a lubricant to the hard excreta formed by a dog which ate the skin and bones of its prey as well as the softer flesh. With softer present-day intake our dogs tend to pass a softer motion and as a result the glands' function is partially lost. This causes the sacs to fill up and stretch the overlying tissue, causing the dog discomfort and making him attempt to get relief by rubbing his bottom on the ground or chewing at his hind-quarters with resultant patches of wet eczema on the skin of the area. The cure in simple cases is by digital compression of the glands and most veterinary surgeons if asked will demonstrate the technique. If the later stages of eczema or abscessing have been reached the appropriate professional advice will have to be sought.

*Bladder*
The urinary bladder, as its name implies, stores the urine. Problems in this organ can be those of inflammation or cystitis with or without bacterial infection, stone-formation within the urine leading to either irritation or blockage of the outlet or urethra, or both conditions together. Correction of all these conditions is essentially the task of the

professional man and, especially in the case of a blockage leading to retention, is urgent in the extreme, requiring a greater or lesser degree of surgical intervention. Cystitis itself may need treatment with bladder antiseptics and antibiotics, as well as adjustment of the diet in order to lessen the chances of recurrences. Urine samples are usually needed to assist in making a positive diagnosis and can easily be obtained from dog and bitch alike if the collection is left to the time at which the animal is most ready to relieve itself. Care should be taken that such samples are collected in dishes and bottles free from all contaminants such as sugar. The actual technique of collection is simplified if an old frying pan is used. In the case of the bitch, give her time to get started before sliding the pan into place, or she may well stop.

*Ears*
The treatment of inflamed ears is without doubt one of the least understood of all first-aid attention required by dogs. It would, as a generalisation, be better if owners were to leave sore ears severely alone rather than attempt to put matters right themselves. The only action that I would suggest for 'home-doctoring' is the use of a little warm olive-oil poured into the canal of the ear in order to assist the dog's attempts to remove wax and other matter which tends to accumulate as the body's response to inflammation. Any attempt at mechanical cleaning, however gently performed, is almost certain to lead to painful and worsening damage to the highly sensitive lining of the external auditory canal. This in turn makes the dog scratch and rub the ear all the more and transforms the mild case into the chronic. There are so many causes of otitis that a proper examination and diagnosis must be made before effective treatment can be instituted.

*Eclampsia*
This condition occurs in the nursing bitch as a result of lowering of the calcium levels in the bloodstream. The usual time of appearance is about two to three weeks after whelping when the bitch is producing the greatest quantity

of milk, but cases are seen from the last week of pregnancy onwards. The symptoms are characteristic, and include rapid breathing, muscular tremors, progressing to inco-ordination and collapse. Total loss of consciousness may be rapidly followed in untreated cases by death, and help should be gained with the utmost urgency.

*Ecto-parasites*
This category includes the four main outside invaders which attack the dog's skin, namely, fleas, lice, mites and ticks. All four are unnecessary and every effort should be made to remove not only the parasites on the body itself but also those which have temporarily detached themselves and are in bedding, kennel-walls and the like. The dog-flea can jump prodigious distances and is not fussy about the species to be used as a host; so it may well land on human skin as well as rabbits, hedgehogs and cats. There are numerous effective products on the market, but it is imperative that whatever is used should be employed exactly according to the makers' instructions (which will usually include warnings about keeping substances away from the animal's eyes). Incidentally, unless the label mentions cats specifically, it is better to assume that it is NOT safe as cats are notoriously susceptible to parasiticides. Lice do not move about with anything like the rapidity of the flea, tending to crawl slowly if they move at all, but they are equally capable of getting off the dog and hiding in cracks and crevices. They are particularly fond of attaching in the folds of skin at the rear edge of the ears and may well be missed as a cause of the dog scratching at its ears. In the cases of both fleas and lice as well as mites, the best method of dealing with those which are off the dog's body in kennels is to use a blow lamp on all surfaces before carrying out the usual cleaning with disinfectant agents.

  Mites are the basic cause of manges. The common sarcoptic mange (scabies) is capable of great resistance to treatment even with the most modern of drugs. It most frequently attacks the areas of skin with least hair on them and these are obviously under the elbows and in the groin. Spread is usually rapid to other parts of the body,

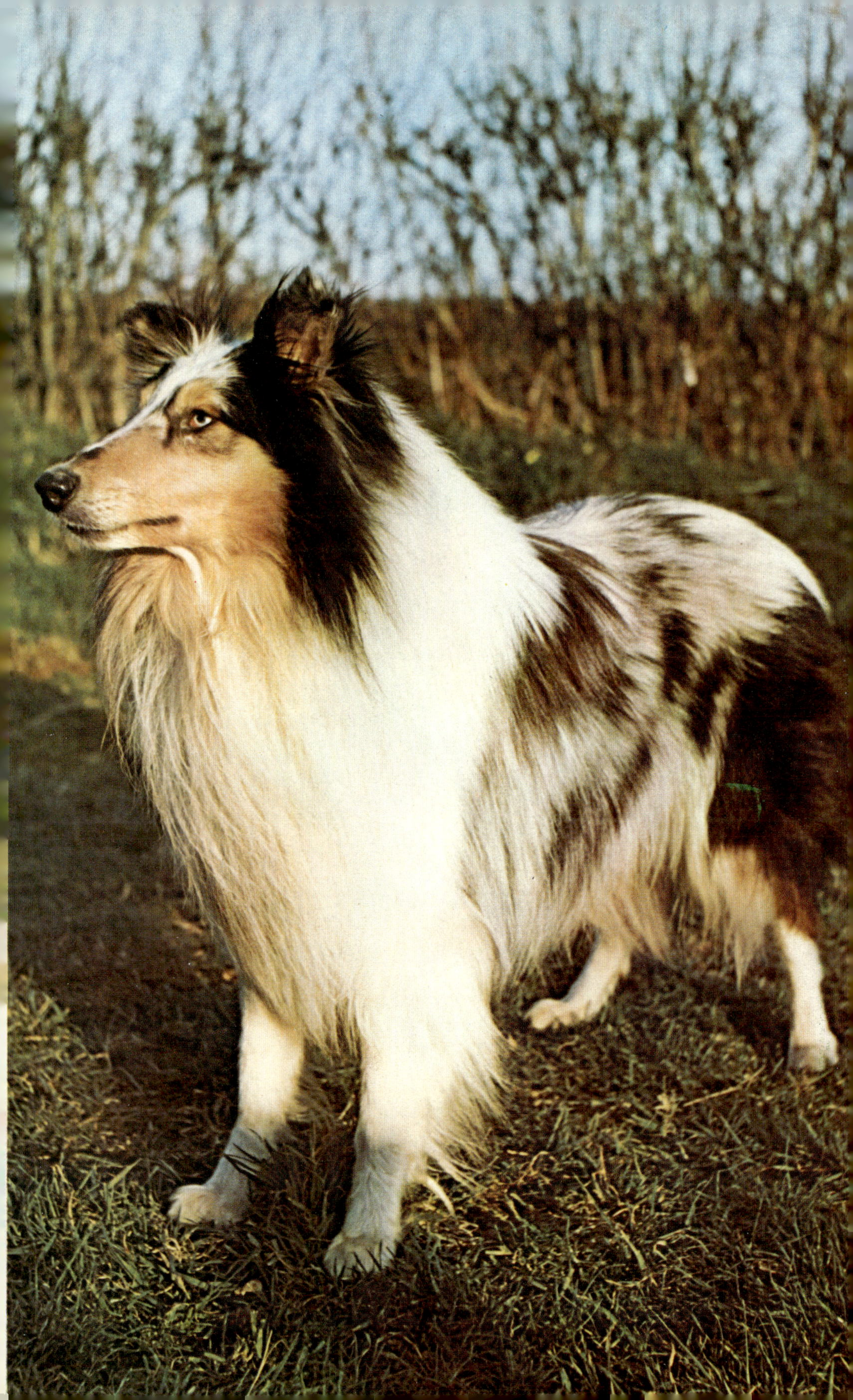

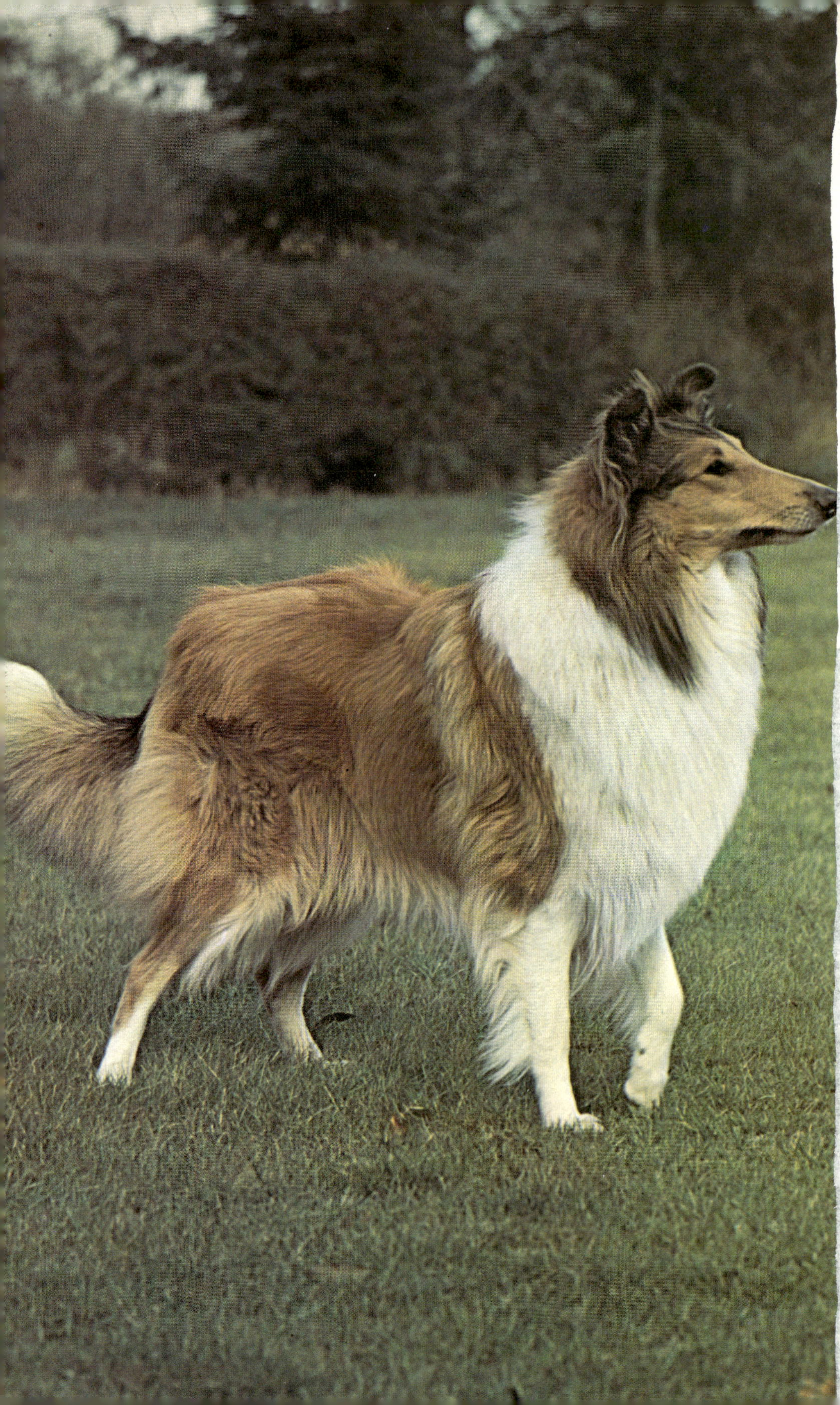

and also to human beings. Treatment under veterinary supervision is essential. Demodectic mange is seen most commonly in the short coated breeds and is associated with congenital infection. The body seems to have some degree of natural resistance to the mite and symptoms in the form of bald areas are first seen at times of stress such as teething in the puppy, heat-periods and whelping in the bitch; in other words the moments when the resistance is at its lowest ebb.

Mites are also found in dogs' ears, the otodectic mange mites, and these are much more common as a source of ear irritation than is generally realised. It is usual to find that the origin of the infection is a cat living in the same household, so it is advisable to treat the family cat if your dog is found to have otodects.

Ticks are normally found in dogs exercised in fields and do not normally attach in large numbers. They may be removed by bathing in appropriate insecticides, but should not be removed by physically pulling them from the skin; a drop of ether may be used to persuade the offender to let go, but as many ticks are found by the dog's eyes, this may not be possible.

*Eyes*
It is as well to deal with the subject of eyes under two quite separate headings. The first can be dealt with very briefly as it concerns the eye-balls themselves, in other words the actual organs of sight. If at any time it should be suspected that a dog's sight is in any way disturbed or impaired, the animal should be taken as soon as possible to a veterinary surgeon and in many cases to one who specialises in opthalmology. There is no place whatsoever for any attempt at home treatment except in the event of a hot or corrosive substance being poured accidentally onto the surface of the eye. In most cases it is best to wash the eye immediately with warm water rather than trying to make up a physiologically correct solution of saline. Having removed to the best of one's ability the damaging substance, the dog should then be rushed straight to the nearest veterinary surgeon.

The eyelids themselves which enclose the conjunctival sacs around the eyes may well be rubbed or scratched by the dog as a result of inflammation of the conjunctiva (conjunctivitis) and it is amazing how much damage a dog can inflict on itself in this way, and treatment should aim at preventing further injury until professional help can be obtained. Simple bland ointments or eye-washes, suitable for use in human eyes, will be perfectly satisfactory for this purpose, but it is essential that these should only be considered as first-aid methods and no substitute for proper advice and treatment. Eyes are much too easily ruined for life to take any risks by adopting a policy of wait and see.

*Fits*
Any form of fit is a serious matter to the owner and, although often very rapid in both onset and recovery, is none the less frightening to witness, especially when it is the first time a fit has been observed. While the attack is in progress, the animal is best placed in a confined space to reduce the chance of self-damage. It is unlikely that a dog undergoing a fit will bite deliberately, but care should be taken in handling on those occasions where some restraint is necessary to avoid damage to the patient and property. Once the fit has ended, a rest in a darkened room is advisable, and meanwhile veterinary attention should be obtained. Different causes of fits can often be distinguished by use of the readings of an electro-encephalograph and such assistance in diagnosis will enable the veterinary surgeon to recommend an appropriate line of treatment or management of the individual.

*Haemorrhage*
Any bleeding from a cut surface should be controlled as soon as possible without waiting for professional help. Wherever it is practicable a pressure pad should be applied by means of cotton wool and bandages. If the first bandage does not stop the bleeding put another one over the top rather than remove the first. If the bleeding on limbs is severe, a tourniquet may be applied above the wound by means of a bandage put on tightly. This is merely a first-

aid technique and veterinary help should be obtained as soon as possible. Tourniquets should not be left on more than ten minutes without being slackened and reapplied nearer the wound if necessary. Other bleeding points such as those on the body should be treated by holding a pad of cotton-wool firmly in contact with the wound for some minutes. Do not keep removing the pad to see how things are going as this may well dislodge the newly formed clots. If a wound needs stitching it needs stitching as soon as possible, so do not wait till tomorrow, get help now!

*Heatstroke*
Under conditions of extreme heat which are sometimes met with in the backs of cars held up in traffic jams, a dog may well suffer from heatstroke as evidenced by vomiting, rapid breathing, weakness and collapse. The body temperature will rise considerably and treatment must begin immediately. Removal to a cool place is obviously the first step and this should be accompanied by the application of cold water to the head and body either by pouring it over the dog or by immersing the animal in a bath. As soon as the animal shows signs of recovery he should be encouraged to drink and meantime should be dried.

*Kidneys*
The functions of the kidneys are bound up with the elimination of body waste from the blood-stream via the urine. The kidney is a highly complicated filter mechanism. Like all specialised tissues, kidney cells once damaged or destroyed do not repair to their full efficiency. Once their function is lost, they are replaced by fibrous tissue which can take no part in the technical task of the kidney. Many old dogs suffer from varying degrees of nephritis or inflammation of the kidney. While much of this nephritis is caused by a specific infection with Leptospira Canicola, a great deal of extra stress is put on the organs by over-feeding, especially with protein, throughout the dog's life. A great number of dogs in 'good homes' are fed with some degree of over generosity. Giving three pounds of raw meat to four-month-old Alsatian puppies does no good to anyone

but the butcher, and puts a tremendous strain on those organs which have to digest and remove the excess protein, in particular the liver and kidneys. This process repeated over a lifetime will inevitably cause harm. As in the case of cystitis, a sample of urine will be required for aiding diagnosis and it may well be that the veterinary surgeon will wish to take a blood sample to estimate the degree of damage present. Advice on treatment will attempt to ensure that the dog's diet is so adjusted to put as little strain on the kidneys as possible and various prepared diets are available on the market to achieve this purpose.

*Poisoning*
No attempt will be made to discuss this subject in any breadth. Suffice to say that any substance which can possibly act as a poison to a dog should be kept out of his way. If this policy fails and any poisonous substances are eaten by a dog, an emetic should be administered as quickly as possible. Washing-soda or a solution of salt and mustard in water will usually do the trick, but even if vomiting is induced, a veterinary surgeon should be consulted as soon as possible for advice as to what further treatment is needed, if possible taking the packet or its name for his information. If the animal is already seriously affected, it is essential that body warmth be maintained while help is being sought, in order to counteract shock. In this context, blankets and hot-water bottles are commonly used. While on the subject of poisons, it is as well to point out that the commonly held opinion that Warfarin rat poisons are harmless to dogs and cats is entirely wrong.

*Skin Diseases*
Apart from the ecto-parasitic types mentioned elsewhere, there are numerous forms of skin troubles. These include ringworm and bacterial types as well as a host of non-specific conditions. These are the plague of the average veterinary surgeon's existence, and their diagnosis requires considerable expertise. Do not try home cures unless you are certain that you know precisely what you are dealing with.

*Stomach and Intestines*
The whole length of the alimentary canal from mouth to anus can be involved in varying combinations of inflammatory disorders. The obvious symptoms are vomiting, diarrhoea, dysentery and constipation. The dog, being a carnivore and having in the wild a tendency to scavenge from the carcasses of dead animals, is fortunate in being provided by nature with great ease in vomiting. If this were not so, the dog would have a poor chance of survival and in many cases a single spasm of vomiting is nothing out of the ordinary, only a response to a bit of injudicious feeding. In most cases vomiting dogs will tend to drink water to excess and it is advisable to remove unlimited

supplies of water from their reach. If boiled water with glucose added (one tablespoonful to a pint) is made available in small repeated quantities most dogs will retain it. If after a short period the dog has stopped vomiting it is then reasonable to offer farinaceous foods in the form of ordinary semi-sweet human biscuits or sponge-cakes for a day or two. If, however, the vomiting continues when glucose water is tried veterinary attention should be sought.

Diarrhoea may occur as a symptom on its own or, as is often the case, as a sequel to vomiting. Again some basic irritation of the bowel is usually the cause and starvation along with the availability of small amounts of glucose-water will often be sufficient to allow the inflammatory condition to subside of its own accord. If it should continue for more than a day or if blood should appear in either vomit or excreta, veterinary advice is essential. Some forms of acute gastro-enteritis produce a great deal of blood from both ends of the alimentary canal and are occasionally rapidly fatal. Professional help is therefore needed at once, whatever the hour.

Constipation is not normally a problem in the dog which is intelligently fed and exercised. It is usually associated with the ingestion of bones whether deliberately provided or scavenged. It is surprising how often well-meaning neighbours will throw bones over the fence to a dog. The safest rule to follow when feeding bones to a dog is to give nothing other than raw, beef, leg-bones. Cooking removes the gelatine and renders the bones more brittle. These are the sort that splinter and provide ideal fragments to penetrate the bowel and cause fatal peritonitis. When constipation occurs, as evidenced by excessive unproductive straining and sometime vomiting, liquid paraffin is the drug of choice and should be given at the rate of an ounce to a 40 lb dog. If this does not produce a rapid answer, get proper help.

While on the subject of the stomach, mention must be made of that violent emergency, torsion of the stomach and Bloat. The affected dog will show symptoms of acute distress with attempts at vomiting with no result. This is because the twisting of the stomach shuts off the cardiac sphincter at the entrance of the stomach and makes it impossible for the stomach contents to leave the organ in a forward direction. The abdomen becomes rapidly and enormously distended and the dog will very soon collapse. This is possibly the most urgent emergency that can be seen in the dog other than the road accident case, and no time should be lost in getting the animal into the nearest surgery or hospital for immediate remedial steps, preferably getting someone else to telephone ahead and warn that the emergency is on its way.

## Throats

The sore throat syndrome may be the result of pharyngitis or tonsillitis, or it may be the result of traumatic damage by sharp bones or needles. One useful way of telling the difference is that dogs with inflamed throats and tonsils will show difficulty swallowing and make gulping movements frequently, while the one with needle stuck in its tongue will in addition paw frantically at its mouth. Either way, get professional attention and never make any attempt to remove needles and the like yourself. You are far more likely to push them on down the throat. Choking may be caused by a dog swallowing a rubber ball which lodges behind the molar teeth and occludes the windpipe. An attempt must be made to remove the object with fingers and by cutting the ball with scissors to deflate it, but this is usually very near impossible. Another common cause is the stick that is thrown for a dog to retrieve. On occasion the stick will land in the ground rather than on it and the dog will run head-on into the other end. This will often result in a nasty wound at the back of the mouth. If this happens, never ignore the occurrence; have the dog examined professionally immediately as, apart from anything else, this accident causes considerable shock to the dog.

## Uterus

The bitch's uterus is prone to trouble more frequently than that of other domestic animals. This is a result of the very delicate hormonal balance obtaining in the bitch which causes her to suffer false pregnancies almost as a normal state. Unfortunately the theories that breeding from a bitch will have any effect on her future chances of avoiding either the changes of false pregnancy or the various forms of inflammation of the uterus (metritis, pyometra), are not founded on fact. The suggestion that bitches which have never had a litter are more prone to pyometra than those that have is based purely on the fact that a greater percentage of bitches are in the former category. Owners contemplating mating their bitches should forget the idea that it is for the bitches' good and think first of whether there is a potential market for the possible puppies or not.

*Vaccination*
Your own veterinary surgeon will inform you of the course of injections which he or she considers most appropriate for your dog or dogs. The diseases which are normally considered are Distemper, Virus Hepatitis and the Leptospira infections. A course of two injections given at the correct ages will give the best possible chance of conferring immunity, and the best advice is that you should consult your veterinary surgeon not later than when the puppy is eight weeks old. You will also get advice as to the correct timing of booster injections and it is unwise to ignore them.

*Worms*
Until recent years, the worm problem was confined to those types known as round-worms and tape-worms. Now however, there is an increasing incidence of hook-worms and some evidence of whip-worm. It is obviously important to know for certain which particular type is infesting your dog. For this reason it is important to ask your veterinary surgeon to identify a specimen if you are in any doubt as to what it is. Each type of worm needs a different treatment régime and this will include not only dosing the dog with the appropriate remedy, but also dealing with the possibilities of re-infestation. In the case of puppies suffering from the ubiquitous roundworm it is advisable to dose the dam both before breeding from her and once she has weaned the litter.

## Finale

If it appears that throughout these notes I have been leading you and your dogs straight into the consulting-room of your veterinary surgeon, I make no apology. When you own a dog or dogs for the first time make it a policy to find a local veterinary surgeon and consult him or her. After the consultation, follow the advice given. If you do you will soon build up mutual confidence and you will receive credit for any knowledge and expertise you will obviously gain. Knowing when you need help, and knowing when you need it urgently are the two pieces of knowledge which will give you the best chance of keeping your dog healthy. If it is at all possible make a habit of taking your dog to the surgery. Many veterinary practices now run efficient appointment systems and in this way you can see the person of your choice and get the greatest benefit of the full equipment of the practice.


### MICHAEL STOCKMAN

I invited Mr Stockman to write this chapter for many reasons, but mainly because I know that for many years he has been very interested, spent much time, and worked very hard to get breeders and members of the veterinary profession to work together in every possible way for the good of the dog. Mr Stockman qualified from the Royal Veterinary College in 1949, and spent four years in the Royal Army Veterinary Corps in Germany and Malaya training war dogs as guards, patrols, and trackers. The rest of his professional life has been spent in a mixed general practice. He is married to a veterinary surgeon who, in his own words, does all the intelligent work in the practice. He first showed dogs in 1942 by handling for a number of breeders and exhibitors of Golden Retrievers, Irish Setters, and Bulldogs. He bought his first Keeshond in 1946, but only started showing the breed with any purpose in about 1960. Now, however, when business permits, he can be seen at most leading shows around the Keeshond rings.

J.C.

# 8 Kennel Club Breed Standards

## BEARDED COLLIE

*Characteristics.* The Bearded Collie should be alert, lively and self-confident, good temperament essential.

*General appearance.* An active dog with long, lean body, and none of the stumpiness of the Bobtail and which though strongly made, shows plenty of daylight under the body and does not look too heavy. The face should have an enquiring expression. Movement should be free and active.

*Head and skull.* Broad, flat skull with ears set high, fairly long foreface with moderate stop. Nose black except with brown or fawn coats, when brown is permitted.

*Eyes.* To tone with coat in colour, the eyes to be set rather widely apart, big and bright. Eyebrows arched up and forward, but not long enough to obscure the eyes.

*Ears.* Medium size drooping with longish hair, slight lift at the base denoting alertness.

*Mouth.* Teeth large and white, never undershot or overshot.

*Neck.* Must be fair length, muscular and slightly arched.

*Forequarters.* Legs straight with good bone, pasterns flexible without weakness, covered with shaggy hair all round.

*Body.* Fairly long, back level, with flat ribs and strong loins, ribcage both deep and long, shoulders flat, straight front essential.

*Hindquarters.* Legs muscular at thighs, with well bent stifles and hocks, free from exaggeration.

*Feet.* Oval in shape, soles well padded, toes arched and close together, well covered with hair including between the pads.

*Tail.* Set low, should be moderately long with abundant hair or brush, carried low when the dog is quiet, with an upward swirl at the tip, carried gaily when the dog is excited, but not over the back.

*Coat.* Must be double, the under one soft, furry and close, the outer one harsh, strong and flat, free from woolliness or any tendency to curl. Sparse hair on the ridge of the nose, slightly longer on the sides just covering the lips. Behind this falls the long beard. A moderate amount of hair under the chin, increasing in length to the chest.

*Colour.* Slate grey or reddish fawn, black, all shades of grey, brown and sandy, with or without white Collie markings.

*Size.* Ideal height at the shoulder:
    Dogs    21–22 ins.           Bitches   20–21 ins.

## ROUGH COLLIE

*Characteristics.* To enable the Collie to fulfil a natural bent for sheep-dog work, its physical structure should be on the lines of strength and activity, free from cloddiness and without any trace of coarseness. Expression, one of the most important points in considering relative values, is obtained by the perfect balance and combination of skull and foreface; size, shape, colour and placement of eye, correct position and carriage of ears.

*General appearance.* The Collie should instantly appeal as a dog of great beauty, standing with impassive dignity, with no part out of proportion to the whole.

*Head and skull.* The head properties are of great importance and must be considered in proportion to the size of the dog. When viewed from the front or the side the head bears a general resemblance to a well-blunted, clean wedge, being smooth in outline. The skull should be flat. The sides should taper gradually and smoothly from the ears to the end of the black nose, without prominent cheek bones or punched muzzle. Viewed in profile the top of the skull and the top of the muzzle lie in two parallel straight planes of equal length, divided by a slight, but perceptible 'stop' or break. A mid-point between the inside corners of the eyes (which is the centre of a correctly placed 'stop') is the centre of balance in length of head. The end of the smooth, well-rounded muzzle is blunt, but not square. The underjaw is strong, clean-cut and the depth of the skull from the brow to the underpart of the jaw must never be excessive (seep through). Whatever the colour of the dog, the nose must be black.

*Eyes.* These are a very important feature and give a sweet expression to the dog. They should be of medium size, set somewhat obliquely, of almond shape and of dark brown colour, except in the case of blue merles when the eyes are frequently (one or both, or part of one of both), blue or blue flecked. Expression full of intelligence, with a quick, alert look when listening.

*Ears.* These should be small and not too close together on top of the skull, nor too much to the side of the head. When in repose they should be carried thrown back, but when on the alert brought forward and carried semi-erect, that is, with approximately two-thirds of the ear standing erect, the top third tipping forward naturally, below the horizontal.

*Mouth.* The teeth should be of good size, with the lower incisors fitting closely behind the upper incisors; a very slight space not to be regarded as a serious fault.

*Neck.* The neck should be muscular, powerful, of fair length and well arched.

*Forequarters.* The shoulders should be sloped and well-angulated. The fore-legs should be straight and muscular, neither in nor out at elbows, with a moderate amount of bone.

*Body.* The body should be a trifle long compared to the height, back firm with a slight rise over the loins; ribs well-sprung, chest deep and fairly broad behind the shoulders.

*Hindquarters.* The hind legs should be muscular at the thighs, clean and sinewy below, with well bent stifles. Hocks well let-down and powerful.

*Feet.* These should be oval in shape with soles well padded toes arched and close together. The hind feet slightly less arched.

*Gait*. Movement is a distinct characteristic of this breed. A sound dog is never out at elbow, yet it moves with its front feet comparatively close together. Plaiting, crossing or rolling are highly undesirable. The hind legs, from the hock joint to the ground, when viewed from the rear, should be parallel. The hind legs should be powerful and full of drive. Viewed from the side the action is smooth. A reasonably long stride is desirable and this should be light and appear quite effortless.

*Tail*. The tail should be long with the bone reaching at least to the hock joint. To be carried low when the dog is quiet, but with a slight upward swirl at the tip. It may be carried gaily when the dog is excited, but not over the back.

*Coat*. The coat should fit the outline of the dog and be very dense. The outer coat straight and harsh to the touch, the undercoat soft, furry and very close, so close as to almost hide the skin. The mane and frill should be very abundant; the mask or face, smooth, also the ears at the tips, but they should carry more hair towards the base; the forelegs well feathered, the hind legs above the hocks profusely so, but smooth below. Hair on the tail very profuse.

*Colour*. The three recognised colours are sable and white, tri-colour and blue merle.

*Sable*. Any shade from light gold to rich mahogany or shaded sable. Light straw or cream colour is highly undesirable.

*Tri-colour*. Predominantly black with rich tan markings about the legs and head. A rusty tinge in the top coat is highly undesirable.

*Blue Merle*. Predominantly clear, silvery blue, splashed and marbled with black. Rich tan markings to be preferred, but their absence should not be counted as a fault. Large black markings, slate colour, or a rusty tinge either of the top or undercoat are highly undesirable.

*White markings*. All the above may carry the typical white Collie markings to a greater or lesser degree. The following markings are favourable: white collar, full or part; white shirt, legs and feet; white tail tip. A blaze may be carried on muzzle or skull or both.

*Weight and size.* Dogs 22–24 inches at shoulder, bitches 20–22 inches. Dogs 45–65 lbs., bitches 40–55 lbs.

*Faults.* Length of head apparently out of proportion to body; receding skull or unbalanced head to be strongly condemned. Weak, snipy muzzle; domed skull; high peaked occiput, prominent cheek bones; dish-faced or Roman-nosed; under-shot or over-shot mouth; missing teeth; round or light coloured and glassy or staring eyes are highly objectionable. Body flat-sided, short or cobby; straight shoulder or stifle; out at elbow; crooked forearms; cow-hocks or straight hocks, large, open or hare feet; feet turned in or out; long, weak pasterns; tail short, kinked or twisted to one side or carried over the back; a soft, silky or wavy coat or insufficient undercoat; prick ears, low-set ears; nervousness.

## SMOOTH COLLIE

(The Smooth Collie only differs from the Rough in its coat, which should be hard, dense and quite smooth.)